Joint Custody & Co-Parenting

Sharing your child equally

A source book
for the separated or divorced family

by
Miriam Galper

Running Press
Philadelphia, Pennsylvania

Canadian representatives: John Wiley & Sons Canada, Ltd.
22 Worcester Road, Rexdale, Ontario M9W 1L1

International representatives: Kaiman & Polon, Inc.
2175 Lemoine Avenue, Fort Lee, New Jersey 07024

9   8   7   6   5   4   3   2   1
Digit on the right indicates the number of this printing.

LIBRARY OF CONGRESS CATALOGING IN PUBLICATION DATA

Galper, Miriam, 1940–
Joint custody and co-parenting.
Edition for 1978 published under title: Co-parenting.
Bibliography: p.
Includes index.
1. Children of divorced parents—United States.
2. Custody of children—United States.
3. Parent and child.
I. Title
HQ777.5.G34   1980   306.8′7   80–21185
ISBN 0–89471–116–4 library binding
ISBN 0–89471–117–2 paperback

Cover art direction by James Wizard Wilson
Cover photography by Carl Waltzer
Cover painting by Nicole Betancourt
Interior design by Peter John Dorman

Printed and bound by Port City Press, Baltimore, Maryland
Typography: Paladium, by CompArt, Inc., Philadelphia, Pennsylvania

This book may be ordered directly from the publisher.
Please include 50 cents postage.

Try your bookstore first.

Running Press
125 South Twenty-Second Street
Philadelphia, Pennsylvania 19103

Foreword

Co-Parenting is a challenging book for divorced or separated parents looking for an alternative approach to raising children. The co-parenting plan permits both parents to remain equally responsible for their children as they maintain separate homes and pursue separate lives. They share custody; they divide time and parenting tasks equally; they remain in a primary relationship with their children. The novelty of the plan lies with the parents' establishing and maintaining a working relationship with each other for their children's sake.

As a practicing psychotherapist, I watch with considerable alarm the pressures on the members of families experiencing separation and divorce. Our society is complex and subject to heavy stress. The nuclear family tries, against mounting odds, to survive in relative isolation. But it is collapsing under the strain. One out of every three marriages ends in divorce; second divorces are becoming more numerous; other marriages deteriorate into chronic unhappiness. So new approaches are needed to family, marital, even post-marital relations. *Co-Parenting* is a pioneer effort in the right direction.

The unwritten rules of divorce behavior are simply horrid. Separating "parties" *should* communicate only through their lawyers. They *must* try to gain whatever advantage they can at the expense of the other. Children *ought* to live with their mothers, and formal visitation rights ought to be arranged for fathers. Ex-couples can *never* be friends and, after divorce, should have as little personal contact as possible.

Well, the rules don't work. They make everyone miserable. But it is difficult to break out of socially sanctioned routines. As a professional, I see a genuinely hopeful prospect in Miriam Galper's approach. The key to the book is this: Ms. Galper stresses the management of the continuing *family* after the breakup of the marriage. She explains, in *Co-Parenting*, how to develop a working relationship with one's ex-spouse both for the sake of the children and for the sake of continuing to experience the full benefits of parenthood.

With their marriage dissolved, new trust and communication are based on the Galpers' mutual decision to take on the responsibilities of co-parenting. This is a realistic and altogether convincing proposal. Surely, Ms. Galper is right in saying that we ought to resist present practices: the system seems to force one of the parents—usually the father—into the role of Sunday "treat man." Children who have the love and harmonious attention of both parents are richer for it. If divorced parents are mature enough to provide an ongoing family life in spite of the dissolution of their marriage, they will have fulfilled their parenting roles and their children will have been the beneficiaries. Co-parenting, in fact, offers a good model for parents who continue to live together as well.

Unfortunately, professionals are often the last to accept new ideas about family roles and child-rearing practices. But their familiarity with the variety of life styles in different cultures and different times should have sensitized them to the truth that no single or rigid set of guidelines could possibly meet the needs of all people. The frequency of divorce and the clamor of unhappiness in our own society confirm the failure of the prevailing "rules." *Co-Parenting* explores a new direction. Professionals ought to take notice. It's certainly clear that children need security, the security of the family. *Co-Parenting* shows how they can find that security in two homes as well as one.

Clorinda G. Margolis, Ph.D.
Associate Professor of Psychiatry
and Human Behavior
Thomas Jefferson University

Contents

Author's Note

From the beginning, I knew that I wanted this book to include the experiences of friends who were co-parenting, reactions of family members, and what professionals had to say about co-parenting. I wrote to over one hundred people, requesting their contributions. Many people responded eagerly. As one friend said, "It's kind of neat to think that how I live and the struggles I've gone through to work out co-parenting might be of use to somebody else." Some people preferred to talk about their experiences rather than write them down. So I interviewed many people—people I knew, people I had heard of who were co-parenting, and professionals I knew who either approved of or were opposed to co-parenting.

My intention was to get a broad spectrum of opinion on the subject. I spoke with people for whom co-parenting was working well and had been since the day they separated. For others, it has been a difficult experience, but one which they felt was worthwhile pursuing. I have used first names only to identify the sexes of the people I spoke with; and, when requested, aliases were used. What you see in italics are excerpts from interviews I conducted and quotations from letters people wrote.

I have not written in detail about co-parenting as it affects teenagers; most of the families I spoke with had children who were age 13 and younger. As these young people become adolescents their concerns in relation to co-parenting will change. Our ability as parents to be flexible in responding to our children's changing needs will determine the success of our co-parenting model. For now, what I have seen is that co-parenting works as well for teenagers as it does for younger children.

I have used the pronoun *he* throughout the book, with the full realization that *he* does not include all the *she's* of the world. Similarly, the term *ex-spouse* does not adequately define the relationship you had with the person you used to be married to. I am asking you to accept these limitations.

It has been exciting for me to write this book. When I first began to co-parent four years ago, I didn't know any other separated couples who chose to share equally in raising their children. Now I do, and the support and acknowledgment that I have received for co-parenting, and for writing this book, have been very satisfying to me. I have had the opportunity to share myself with others and I am grateful to all the people who have contributed to my life by sharing themselves with me.

M.K.G.
Bryn Mawr, Pa., 9 January 1978

THREE YEARS LATER
A Preface to the Revised Edition

Three years have passed since I wrote this book. Many circumstances of my life have changed, yet much has remained the same. Jeff and I are still co-parenting and have smoothed out the old logistical problems, but because of the changes in our lives we have discovered new problems. We have both moved to Center City Philadelphia, two blocks apart, and because Josh is now 10½, he is the one who picks up things that he might have left at the other parent's house. He is his own drop-off and delivery service, and he moves back and forth between the two homes easily. He carries around not one, but two sets of keys, and seems proud to have them both with him at all times.

Our schedule is now different from the one I described in the first edition of this book. When I first wrote the book I interviewed many families and heard about different schedules. I was amazed at the variety of schedules and impressed by the ways that families figured out what worked for them—and I heard about a schedule that sounded better than the one we had. For several years, Jeff, Josh, and I felt that three and a half days was not a long enough stretch of time together. According to our schedule, neither Jeff nor I ever had a whole weekend off or a whole weekend to do something with Josh without special permission from the other parent. So, we changed our schedule and it has been working well. We now operate in a two-week time frame. Josh is with Jeff every Monday and Tuesday night, with me every Wednesday and Thursday, and we alternate weekends, so that every other week one of us has a five-day stretch of time with Josh, while the other has a five-day stretch of time without him. Every other weekend I'm with Josh from Wednesday through Monday morning. We can go away together, or we can just hang out for long periods of time. And then on my weekend off, I can do things I enjoy doing by myself.

Joshua goes to school in Center City Philadelphia, across the street from my home, and three blocks from Jeff's. Many of the children in his school come from separated or divorced families, and co-parenting is accepted. I did not have to educate Joshua's teachers about it. I asked that notices be sent to both me and Jeff. To date, we have not had an incident where one parent felt left out or one parent didn't know what was going on at school. I just received a Registration Form from Josh's school and there is a section which reads, "If the natural parents of the child are divorced or separated, please complete the rest of this section. With whom does the child live? If this is a shared situation, please elaborate." And it goes on to ask who should be invited to parent/teacher conferences, who should receive mailings from the school, and so forth. Further, Josh's living situation is no longer so different from that of his classmates. Many of his friends live with one parent for part of the time and the other parent the rest of the time. The school directory lists both my phone number and Jeff's, so it is easy to tell a child who calls that Josh is at his Dad's house and to call there. Josh's friends want to be with *him*; they don't really care which house he's at, and they are willing to make another phone call to find him.

From time to time, a discussion will come up about a child deciding that he wants to live with one parent permanently after a number of years of living with both parents in two homes. When Josh hears that, he is quick to add his opinion—there is "no way" he wants to do that. He wants to keep being with both me and his Dad. That isn't to say that he is pleased with our arrangement all the time, but on the whole co-parenting has worked out for Josh. It has been going on for seven years, and it is no longer our noble experiment in living.

A factor which *has* changed our lives is that Jeff and Barbara, who lived together for several years, were recently married. My relationship with them has become a very close one. Barbara and I have developed a friendship that is independent of Jeff, and we consider each other to be in the "best friends" category. It took a willingness from each of us to communicate with the other, to keep in touch, to be open with each other—even when it felt ugly or difficult. We seem to be in one of those difficult times right now, and it is due to Barbara and Josh's relationship, which has not been a smooth one. There are good times for them, to be sure, but there are also times when they dislike each other immensely. Jeff expects Josh's schedule to continue even if he is out of town—Josh can stay with Barb and her son Ricky. However, neither Barb nor Josh has that expectation, so there has been some upset and confusion about roles.

A stereotype that causes problems for many stepfamilies is the notion that family members are supposed to love each other. But the experience of family counselors in social agencies, and the literature in the field, shows that this is just not so. People may grow to love one another, but it is unlikely that there will be deep love between stepparents and stepchildren. As a result, we are now re-examining some of the assumptions we had about co-parenting and what our roles in the situation are.

Perhaps we are facing the problems of all blended families: who is part of what family; how does it feel for the spouse of the person who is co-parenting; what are the difficulties when one child moves in and out of the home, while other children are there all the time; and so on. We are looking again at whether this arrangement works for all of us, and if not, what changes we want to make. I find this frightening. My world is fairly settled and a large part of me wants it to stay like that. But another part wants to continually explore options, to question what is best, to look at Joshua's changing needs as he gets older, and be willing to go with whatever seems appropriate at the time. All we all can do is to go from right now and make our lives, and our children's, the way we want them to be. That takes work, communication, a willingness to hear what might be unpleasant, and a commitment to work things out. It always does.

One example of this is the feelings I had about Jeff and Barb's wedding. I'll describe them to you because I think the experience illustrates the joys and problems of being closely connected to people with whom one is not supposed to feel closely connected. Somehow, I sensed that it was coming. Jeff and Barb and I were at a friend's wedding, sitting at the same table, and I turned to them and said I thought they would get married soon. They laughed and didn't agree or disagree. But within a few weeks, Jeff called to say that it was so. I was pleased for them. I was impressed by their commitment to each other, and I knew what they had gone through to want to be married. There had been a lot of ups and downs in their relationship, and I admired the fact that they stuck with each other and worked things out.

The question of where they were to be married came up, who would marry them, who would be there—the usual wedding issues. It was my suggestion that was finally acted on—they would get married in their own home (they had been living together for a year and a half in a home they had bought together), and close friends and family would come to the ceremony, which would be followed by an open house. I didn't stay posted on all the details, and I realized later that Barb was protecting me and didn't think I'd be interested. We did talk about the invitations, and I suggested that a group of friends come over to do them. I'd organize the assembly line, Barb could serve lunch, and everything could be accomplished in a few hours. That was a very strange day for me. I wrote invitations to Jeff's relatives—the same ones who had come to *my* wedding. I think I went over the line on that one—my line, for what I could handle.

About two weeks before the wedding, I noticed that I was very upset. I was crying a lot. I was staying away from Jeff and Barb. Yet everything was focused around "the wedding." I ran around getting wedding clothes for Josh. Jeff's brother was arriving from Seattle and was going to stay with me, as was my friend Caroyln from Milwaukee. In short, I was a mess. I called a therapist whom I had seen several years before and spent two hours with her, mostly crying. She told me to have compassion for myself. I wanted to be so big about it all, so strong, so invincible. I didn't want to own up to the slightest bit of pain about the event, and yet I was unhappy about it. As the wedding day drew near, I couldn't wait for it. I wanted it to be over.

The day before the wedding, I went scurrying around trying to find something to wear in my hair. I had a picture in my mind of what I wanted and couldn't find it anywhere. Finally, I found the perfect thing—pink glass flowers on combs with dangling smaller pink glass flowers. I was also anxious that Josh should look perfect. I had bought him a very snazzy sports jacket—he had never owned one before—and real shoes, not sneakers. I had thoughts of myself being like Jackie Kennedy at the funeral. And it *was* a dying of sorts to me, a dying of some special part of my relationship with Jeff. I also thought there was some shift in Jeff's relationship with Josh. Who was number one? Now it was Barbara, it seemed.

On the morning of the wedding, Jeff and Barb came over to my house to tape some music they wanted, and we all just hung around. It seemed so easy and convivial, and natural, that they should be at my house on that day. When Josh and I left the house, it was a magnificent spring day. The neighbors were out, and they smiled at us, never having seen us so decked out together before. I didn't tell them where we were going, but Josh and I chuckled about that. I walked tall.

There was some toasting after the ceremony, and one of the things I said was how proud I was of us all. And that remains true. We have developed an unusually close relationship, and that has had its difficulties for me. Sometimes I feel left out, excluded at critical times. I don't want to be married to Jeff, yet I miss the closeness we shared. I was alone at the wedding, I took care of myself, my friends took care of me, Jeff's mother and relatives admired me and Barb's family and friends were wonderful to be with. With all that, I joyously celebrated their marriage. Our relationship was special, intimate. We had fun together. I teared up once or twice during the ceremony; I felt loving toward people; I felt pretty. It was strange sometimes, and I would not have missed it for anything.

However, it was also difficult. There are no books of etiquette, or a chapter even, to describe what the ex-wife of the groom should wear. Does she appear in the family wedding shot? The photographer, my friend Ira, asked all the Galpers to gather together for a picture. My name is Galper, but am I *really* a Galper? I ended up being in the picture. We have no social norms for these occasions. I was part of the family, and I wasn't. I am, and I'm not. And we have no names to describe our relationships.

Barbara and I are more than friends; sometimes we think of ourselves as sisters. There is a kinship and a connectedness that has no name. The ease in my being with Jeff and Barb has a lot to do with Barbara and her special qualities as a person. Almost from the beginning, she has encouraged Jeff and me to remain close. If Jeff and I are feeling distant from each other or seem to be bickering, it is Barbara who will suggest that Jeff and I spend some time together. She understands that we can be a support to each other, that we are friends, and that doesn't threaten her in her relationship with Jeff. Barbara includes me in her home, in her family. She makes room for me in a way that makes me feel very comfortable, and that has been very special for me. I know how difficult this has been for her at times, and I admire her a great deal.

And what about Barb's son? We don't spend a whole lot of time together, yet he is more to me than just another friend of Joshua's. He and Josh are step-brothers. What does that make him to me? And what about Barb's parents? I feel close to them and to her brothers, and they've taken me in as one of their own. What am I to them? Their ex-daughter-in-law? Their son-in-law's ex? Barbara's ex-in-law? HELP!

It's not just that there are no names. There are no norms, and that is what makes all this difficult. In these new relationships, we are on uncharted territory, new ground. We are exploring the terrain for the first time. It feels awkward, exciting, and very demanding. People are watching.

I was looked at a lot at the wedding. Not in a nasty way, but with curiosity. How would she take it? Would she hold up? Sometimes I can take it, and sometimes it all feels too much for me. After all, I grew up with certain fundamental beliefs, certain traditional values, and they are still with me. I've internalized the way I think the social order should be. I may fight it, or intellectualize about the new freedom in relationships and consider myself a part of the human potential movement and the social revolution—but all that is countered by the tremendous pulls of my socialization, which says you stay married, that to divorce is scandal, and that you have to hate your ex-husband's new wife.

But the social order *is* changing. The typical American family is more myth than reality. Today, typical American family life might include divorce, a remarriage or two, children from previous marriages—my children, his children, our children, various in-laws, ex-laws, and so on. How are we all to get along? No rules, no books. Therapy groups are now springing up in social agencies for what is known as blended, or reconstituted families (I am always reminded of orange juice when I hear those terms). It is now a subspecialty in the human service field—how to work with families that are more than the sum of their parts.

What keeps families together are the children. It is the children who demand without saying it that we be true to our ideals of parenting, of being mature, responsible adults. Co-parenting says to our children that we will not make them choose between one parent or another and that we, as parents, will both continue to respond to their needs, to care for them and nurture them. I think we owe our children a decent life, and that means being decent to people with whom it might be difficult to deal. It may be unrealistic of me, but I don't care about the bitterness and anger that people hold onto for years. Sure, it's there, but we can't allow it to run us. It is just too damaging to our kids, not to mention ourselves.

People are working out new arrangements, new ways of relating to each other, and the possibilities are endless. New forms of family life are being created, and none of them may match our image of what the family is supposed to be. My family has really been me and Josh and Jeff and Barb and Rick. They have been my central force, the people I celebrate holidays with, the people I have dinner with more often than anyone else. For my friend Carolyn, her family includes her lover and her child, her child's father, his lover, his lover's son, and the son's father.

In this situation, co-parenting has been the raison d'être for developing the relationships in the first place. But I doubt that co-parenting forced those kinds of relationships upon us. Rather, it was our need to remain related and connected that led us to develop co-parenting.

There is no one out there who can say what is the right or wrong way to handle relationships after separation and divorce. Certainly what works for me may not for you. But I'd venture to say you don't know the half of what's available to you in the ways you can relate to your ex-spouse. Have you closed the doors? Are you positive you have nothing more to say to the person with whom you created a child? And what about the woman he's married to now, who spends a lot of time with your child? Aren't there things that you would like to talk to her about? Who says that you have to hate that woman? Sometimes it's easier to have enemies in life, to know for sure who's right and who's wrong. It doesn't create anxiety that way, anyhow.

I'd like to close with a few words on what this book has meant to me. I am amazed, surprised, and thrilled when I get calls or letters from people who tell me how much reading *Co-Parenting* has contributed to their lives. Some people have copied exact schedules from the book, some have given the book to their spouse as a way of explaining what they want after a separation. In general, people are grateful to read about an alternative to traditional custody arrangements.

From time to time, I appear on radio and television to discuss co-parenting. In April, 1978, I was on "The Phil Donahue Show" and faced an audience that was fairly hostile and closed to the whole idea. The main reaction from the audience seemed to be that children belonged with their mothers, that fathers didn't know how to take care of children, and that it was vaguely unAmerican for a mother not to want to be with her child twenty-four hours a day, seven days a week. In July, 1980, I appeared on a television talk show in Detroit called "Taylor Made." The audience was receptive and open, there were several men there who had full custody of their children, and there were children of divorced families who asked very moving questions. My experiences on these two programs have shown that times have certainly changed. People are much more aware of the issue; movies like *Kramer vs. Kramer* have brought the issue into the spotlight. Both *Newsweek* and *Time* have run articles on joint custody, and it is no longer the unknown bugaboo it once was. The problem of separation and divorce has grown in this country, not lessened. It didn't go away as some people hoped, and more and more the old ways are just that—old.

I've shared a lot of my doubts with you, my apprehensions and uncertainties, and my growing pains. That's really how I see all this *sturm und drang*—growing pains. It's the growth and development of a new way to live, this joint custody. Any way we choose to live is not perfect, and there are always unresolved areas for us to work on and brood about, to make us wonder if we're doing the right thing. So, too, with joint custody.

In the traditional ways of separation and divorce, much of the psychological work people need to do involves working out ways of coping with loss. I have had to do that too, to be sure, but I've also had another framework, and that is coping with additions. The additions are; Jeff, Barb and her son Rick, and Barb's whole family. So it hasn't all been unhappy or unpleasant. Much of the closeness with them, and my continued co-parenting with Jeff, has produced enormous pleasure and satisfaction for me. I am generally pleased with the way I live, and pleased that Josh has not had to give up one iota of either parent. He is so close to Jeff that I have no doubts that joint custody was right for us.

The progressions and changes that we have been through did not just happen to get us to where we are right now. These changes merely get us to the next level, where we change some more, go through more transitions, more pleasures, more disequilibrium from time to time. That's just the way it is. The context for me has been sharing my child equally—being a responsible co-parent. And no matter what changes are made in our routines or our schedule, Jeff and I will always be co-parents. I'm certain of that. And Josh will never have to wonder about his parents' love for him. He knows it, he gets it. We have proved it to him, if indeed we ever had to.

M.K.G.
Philadelphia, 1980

*My marriage has ended and my family
continues. This book is dedicated to my
ex-husband Jeffry and my son Joshua.*

Introduction: What Is Co-Parenting?

From the minute we decided to separate, we knew that co-parenting was automatic for us. It seemed a very natural, human way to behave, just an accepted thought—like, "You get the piano, I get the decorated blanket chest, we co-parent."

Larry Teacher

Jeff and I were married in August, 1965. He was 23, I was 25.

Joshua was born in January, 1970.

Jeff and I separated in February, 1974.

We were divorced in May, 1976.

The dates seem cold and don't reveal that we are still family to one another. The father of my son will always be related to me because of our commitment to co-parenting. Our involvement with each other is ongoing. Jeff and I have been sharing the child-rearing activities since we separated; for us, this seemed like a natural outgrowth of the way we lived as a nuclear family. After a number of years now co-parenting has evolved into our way of life.

Co-parenting is a method of child raising that you may want to consider after a separation or divorce takes place. It is sometimes called joint custody, joint parenting, co-custody, or shared custody. What all these terms have in common is the assumption on the part of both parents that neither one has ownership (custody) of the children. This is not necessarily a legal agreement, but can be a moral one. Co-parenting requires a relationship between parents that is based on trust and respect for each other, and one in which there is some degree of harmony.

Co-parenting means that the children spend approximately equal amounts of time with each parent; tasks related to child rearing are divided between both parents in a way that makes sense to them; and major decisions are made jointly concerning the health and well-being of the children. Co-parenting is an attitude on the part of both parents that they are intimately connected to one another through their children and that they respect the other's relationship with those children. This means that one parent does not have the right to move to another city and automatically expect to take the children along. That might indeed happen, but only as a result of a decision mutually arrived at.

There are a lot of gray areas involved in the definition of co-parenting, and I don't want to get into a struggle about who co-parents and who doesn't. Some people feel that they co-parent even though the time they spend with their children is far from equal. For these people, a shared sense of responsibility may transcend time allotments. But by any definition, both parents are involved in the daily routines of living with their children. Both have days when they get up early with their children, pack lunches, get them off to school, talk to teachers, drive to piano lessons, and days that are defined as play times. Both parents are responsible for taking care of a sick child, for making dentist appointments, for refilling the vitamin prescription, for buying new sneakers. These tasks can be divided in some way. What is important in co-parenting is that both parents assume a responsibility for meeting a share of all the physical needs, as well as the financial and emotional needs, of their children.

Co-parenting is feasible no matter how many children you

have. Two or three children, as well as one, can move back and forth between two homes. Of course, whether you are co-parenting or living in an intact family, the more children you have the more arrangements you will need to make. Co-parenting with more than one child has no special set of rules; you may arrange your schedule so that you spend time with your children either separately or all together (or both ways, on an alternating basis).

Co-parenting means sharing your children equally. It is a creative method of child raising that I encourage you to consider as an alternative to the more traditional custody arrangements in which one parent has custody of the child and the other parent, usually the father, has visitation rights. When parents share equally in caring for a child, even though they are separated or divorced, that child experiences his parents' love for him.

Love for him means that his parents are willing to go through all kinds of time and effort to process things. I think that's a wonderful way to look at what love is; it will support the child very well in relationships that he forms himself. I don't think a child raised in this kind of situation will ever be able to be glib about a human relationship, or lazy about it—because it will be built into his mind that part of loving somebody is being willing to put in that kind of time and effort to make things work. [Roslyn]

This child does not equate separation of his parents with being abandoned by one of them. Mother and father both remain active as parents; each remains supportive of the other in the joint effort to work out the many facets of child rearing. Neither parent is alone with the responsibility of raising the children.

One of the first areas of responsibility that needs to be resolved after separation takes place is financial. To me, sharing in Joshua's financial support was always important. Just as I am responsible for taking care of his physical needs, I am responsible for providing for him financially. Yet it is generally not realistic to talk about an equally divided arrangement, since

17

most men make more money than most women. What seems more feasible is an arrangement in which proportions of support are pro-rated according to the income of each parent. For instance, if the father makes $12,000 per year and the mother earns $8,000, then he would pay 60% of a child's costs and she would pay 40%, since he earns 20% more than she. However these matters get worked out, the principle is the same: the responsibility for financial support is shared to whatever extent possible.

I am often asked how much money Jeff gives me in child support. The answer is nothing. I do not get child support and the very notion of that question upsets me, since it assumes that I do not support my son and that his father does—which is clearly not the case. Financial arrangements can be easy to work out once you have established a principle to work with; and they will be easy to work out if the woman has a steady job, especially if it is one at which she has been working throughout the marriage. All too often, however, that is not the case.

Many women curtail their potential careers in order to keep home and hearth together. Many have little or no income of their own, have no marketable skills, and are totally dependent on their husbands for financial support. How can these women possibly share responsibility for financial support of the child? They cannot, obviously. What they can do, in an agreement made with their husbands, is plan how long it will take them to become self-supporting, and get support for themselves and their children until this is accomplished. For instance, you may include in your separation agreement that you, mother, will go back to school to get your degree, or participate in a job training program, during which time your husband will provide for you and the children as he did before. When you complete your training, his support will decrease as your earnings increase, and you will be able to work out a new financial agreement based upon your new earning capacity.

One of the major tasks facing any newly separated woman is planning to become financially independent. Some men will be more open to the idea of support which is limited in time, rather than support which seemingly has no end. I think it's important to state your willingness to take financial responsibility for yourself and for your share of the children's costs. Women who do this feel good about themselves.

We never had money problems and we don't have money problems now. Larry has agreed to take care of all of Rachael's costs. I'm sorry I can't do more. I would like to be in a position to split the tuition, split the camp, do everything on a fifty-fifty basis. I figure that in the next couple of years I'll be able to achieve it. I hope so. It would make me feel good to pay my share of my daughter's costs. [Marilynn]

A positive attitude toward sharing financial responsibilities is important to successful co-parenting.

Trust and respect between the parents are also key ingredients. Co-parents should be on good terms with each other and have a sense of how to communicate with each other. This takes time to develop. Just after a separation, there are very few couples who are on good working terms. Yet they do have a sense of wanting to be civil toward each other, especially where the children are involved. They know they don't want to use the children to work out any struggle they might have between them. Co-parenting will not work unless both parents can deal with each other as mature adults who are no longer married but who have a child to care for. It is complicated and necessary to end the spouse system while maintaining the parent system. Before deciding whether you want to co-parent, examine your feelings about yourself and your ex-spouse. Are you feeling vindictive toward your ex-spouse? Do you want revenge? Do you think of not giving your ex what he or she wants—the child—because you felt rejected and you want to retaliate? It's okay if you have these feelings—but what are you going to do with them? Act on them, or recognize you have them and move on? If you choose to act on them, then you should probably not choose co-parenting. This system needs sincere cooperation and trust between the parents in order for it to work.

Co-Parenting

After Bruce and I got less estranged and became more like friends, I remember being able to call him up and talk to him about problems I was having with Jonathan. This was a real breakthrough to be able to do this. Now we don't hesitate to get together and talk about problems that come up. I think you have to have some shared values as co-parents. People are breaking up marriages for different reasons than they used to. They may still like each other and share similar values. Bruce and I started out with different values and came around to sharing more and more. [Ann]

On the other hand, I know of some parents who do not talk to each other regularly although they do co-parent. They do not share in discussions about the child's emotional well-being and they communicate with each other only when absolutely necessary. Their system works for them. They know themselves well enough to know that they need to stay away from each other as much as possible. They are committed to co-parenting and have not used their anger at each other in a destructive manner.

There's some kind of basic trust and respect for each other that Bob and I don't have. Oh, I respect the relationship my kids have with him because I know that he loves them. But in terms of being together in how we perceive the kids and how we want to deal with them, that's something else. We are very, very different parents. We each raise them very separately. If a problem came up with one of the kids in school, I might discuss it with Bob but I would know that he would deal with it in his way and I'd do it my way. He hates the way I deal with the kids. But we don't have fights or running battles about things—it's not like that. On the other hand, it's not like it could be. We don't work out stuff about the kids, we don't plan for them together. Oh maybe a little bit, but on the stuff that doesn't really count. Like Christmas. We'll cooperate on who's going to buy them what. But in terms of major values, what kind of people we want our kids to be, we're miles apart. So we let each other go our separate ways. [Jennifer]

Whether or not your basic values differ, you need to keep your agreements with each other. I honor the arrangement that

Jeff and I have worked out quite seriously. I respect the time that Joshua spends with his father and the relationship that they have. Occasionally, I am invited to a function with Joshua that takes place on one of the days that he is usually with Jeff. Depending on the importance of it to me, I will ask Jeff how he feels about my being with Joshua that day. I do not assume that I can arbitrarily change our schedule to suit my convenience. I don't mean to imply that there's no flexibility in our arrangement. There is. But I respect Jeff's feelings about what it would mean for him not to be with Joshua on one of his days, and I am not willing to abuse the privilege of asking that the schedule be changed.

Jeff and I have put a tremendous amount of time and energy into co-parenting. Initially, it seemed that we were spending all our waking hours working out arrangements, talking over Joshua's reactions, planning for his needs, settling financial accounts, and dealing with our own feelings about how much contact we were having with each other at the same time we were working on separating from each other. It was a difficult task and the effort has definitely paid off. Jeff and I and Joshua are very comfortable with our routine now, and with the amount of contact we all have with each other.

For many people, though, the idea of co-parenting seems to be difficult to grasp. I suspect this has to do with the fact that in most families the responsibility for child rearing is usually the mother's. The father is seen as provider or, at best, helper to the mother. Men are assumed to be inadequate when it comes to nurturing—and it is true that men generally have not been trained in the way women have been to be emotionally supportive and giving to children around them. Indeed, it is hard for some people to understand first, that the father may actually *want* to take a more active role in child rearing, and then, that he is actually capable of doing it.

I had no idea what shared custody was. We didn't know how to work this. I was open to it. I think it's the best thing that could have happened to me and my kids. It's like a plus out of a negative ending. I

Co-Parenting

didn't have nearly as good a relationship with my kids as I do now, especially my older daughter. I made a lot of mistakes with her and I didn't spend much time with her when I was married. Now I am with her more. A lot of people envy me. I have the best of both worlds. I'm a parent, I have the kids, and yet I have my own free time too. [Charles]

I am asked over and over again what the quality of the relationship is between my son and his father. I am asked if I worry that my son isn't well taken care of when he is with his father, that his father won't think of getting out the galoshes when it's raining, that my son won't eat properly at his father's house. The concerns people have about Joshua's well-being when he is with his father seem endless to me. I always saw Jeff as a competent father and I get angry when I feel that I should have to defend his right and ability to take care of his own child. The questioning I get centers around Jeff as a man doing a job that women usually do, "women's work," as it is sometimes called.

It is important to me that I am never uneasy about the quality of care Joshua receives when he's with his father. I have to travel periodically as part of my job; if it is on days when Joshua is usually with me, Jeff takes over. When I am out of town, I am often asked who is taking care of my son (I often wonder if Jeff is asked who is taking care of his son when he travels), and when I say he's with his father there's usually some stunned reaction. I get the feeling that it would seem more natural to some folks if I answered that my mother came from out of town to take care of Joshua, instead of Jeff assuming that role.

Our attitude is what allows us to assume extra responsibilities and time with Joshua, should it be difficult to adhere to our usual schedule. This sense of filling in for the other person gives a great freedom of movement; it is very comfortable for me to leave town with the knowledge that Joshua is well cared for. Jeff and I both know Joshua's routines, his best friends, his favorite days in school, and we can take over for the other person without much disruption in any of our lives.

Even with open, cooperative attitudes, however, either parent may for some reason find the idea of co-parenting intimidating. Many men have not had close contact with their children before a separation takes place, and they are naturally apprehensive about their ability to manage with a child alone. They may be unused to spending a lot of time alone with their child and yet know that they do not want to lose frequent contact with their child.

When I first had Aaron by myself, I was very panicked. There were times that I felt I could never do this, that it was foolish for me to try. It took a long time to get over that. When we were alone in the house, it was a very scary thing. When I was married I had taken some responsibility for Aaron; but now there was nobody else to talk to; if I got angry I wouldn't know what to do. [Evan]

If you are a man who has separated, I would like to encourage you just to think about what co-parenting could mean to you. It is natural to be worried and fearful. Parenting is an acquired skill and can be learned through various methods. You can talk to friends, read books, talk with your ex-wife, and you can learn by doing it. You can learn from your own experiences with your child about the best ways for you and your child to develop a relationship, or to continue one, now that you are a single parent. As a co-parent, you will be actively involved in your child's daily life, including his activities at school and with his playmates. You will get to know your child very well, in a way that is usually not possible with only weekend visitation rights. And you probably will be amazed and very pleased as you watch your nurturing skills grow.

Many men realize that, for the system to work, they need to reorder priorities in their lives. When you are considering co-parenting, you may find that advancing your career seems less important than having a job which is flexible enough to allow for active parenting. Can you bring your child to work with you if the sitter gets sick, or the after-school program is closed? Are you able to take a few hours off so you can go to a parent-teacher conference? Can your work schedule accommodate to the surprises that inevitably accompany being responsible for a child?

These questions apply to the mother's job as well. How many people, men or women, have jobs which allow time to fulfill parental responsibilities? Not many. Maybe your answers to these questions are no, I can't leave work whenever something comes up. It is possible to keep a high pressure job and successfully co-parent, or to have a job which is fairly rigid about time requirements, but I think it will be that much harder for you.

Logistically, co-parenting is easy to manage if one parent has a job which allows for a flexible time schedule. This job would tend to be one with less pressure, less responsibility, and less money. For some people, it might be worthwhile to consider alternating periods of time in which one parent has that kind of job, and then the other. This would allow for at least one parent to be especially available to take care of a sick child or attend to any unexpected needs.

Initially, mothers may feel threatened by even the thought of not having their children with them for some period of time. A woman's identity is usually connected with her roles as wife and mother, so that when her marital status changes, motherhood may seem like the only familiar hold on reality. If there's no child at home to cook dinner for, then what is life about? What's the purpose in existing for a woman who has seen herself primarily as a wife and mother and who suddenly has no husband and no child to take care of? How to fill the time if there's no bath to give, no homework to look at, question to answer, or need to be filled? Or if there's no one else home for company? What structure is there for the days, and especially the nights? None, at first, and that is an anxious time that has to be experienced and worked out by each woman in her own way.

These feelings can be just as intense for a woman who has been working outside the home. I remember the first night after Jeff and I separated that Joshua slept at his father's house. I remember walking around my house, just moaning and wondering aloud where everybody was. I felt crazy and that there was no longer any meaning to my life. That may sound melodramatic—yet many newly separated women report similar feelings. When Joshua was with me again I felt overwhelmed by my seemingly endless responsibilities. The routine chores loomed large to me, although I had been used to doing them; there was no relief in sight, and that realization filled me with panic.

Here is the way one friend of mine described her time alone without her children:

Our schedule used to be that I had the kids during the week and Bob took them every weekend. It was like party time for me when they were away, and I was free. Now the schedule is that I have them for two weeks and Bob has them for two weeks and I feel completely different. Now when the kids are with Bob it's not just a vacation for me—it's also learning to live by myself. After the third or fourth day alone, it starts to feel strange—not awful, not like I feel bad or scared or even lonely—just strange. It's a very weird, foreign feeling, to feel that silence closing in around me like that. Yet as much as these feelings do exist at first, they're nothing compared with the advantages of our arrangement, so far as I'm concerned—the advantages of having regular periods of time free from parental chores and being totally in charge of how I spend my time around my house. [Jennifer]

To both parents I want to say that as time passes you will ease into your own routines, learn what is comfortable for you, and forget (almost) how strange it felt in the beginning.

You will be left with a feeling of deep satisfaction in knowing that you can, in fact, take care of your children totally. You will take immense pleasure in the fact that you can handle all kinds of situations competently. You will find your own strengths as a parent and thrive on the special relationship you have with your children. What used to feel difficult, such as the times when a mother is alone without her children, comes to feel like a luxury—the pleasure of child-free time on a regular basis. What used to feel hard for some men, caring for children physically and emotionally, now gives them a wonderful feeling of self worth as they successfully maneuver in the world of parenting.

We are all aware of the increase in the number of marriages that now end in separation or divorce. Over the last decade we have been deluged with books and articles telling us of the pain and suffering, the loss and trauma, that divorce brings. Recently, however, several books have been written about using divorce as a creative force in your life. Divorce is viewed as a vehicle for growth and change and as a chance to evaluate your situation and make some innovative decisions and choices for the future.

"But what about the children?" is a phrase that echoes in the minds of parents and professionals when the subject of divorce comes up. The children are seen as the innocent victims for whom divorce can be only a shattering and crippling experience from which they will never fully recover. These people would say that the loss of a two-parent home equals doomsday. Many of these two-parent homes, however, were de facto one-parent homes, where the mother usually had major, and sometimes total, responsibility for child raising. After separation and divorce, it is still the mother who is expected to remain the custodial parent.

Several forces that have come into play in the last few years have begun to change this pattern. One is the emergence of the second wave of feminism, the women's movement of the late 1960s and early 1970s. Women began to question the role of wife and mother and to want to change the stereotyped husband/father role in which the man is a passive participant in the lives of his children. It was exciting, if threatening, to consider changing the basic assumptions women and men had about themselves and each other. The threatening part was in knowing that for changes to occur, there would have to be some shifts in the power relationships between men and women. And there were no guarantees about how it would all turn out. A woman who had total responsibility for child raising would have to relinquish some control in this area if she really wanted her husband to become an active parent. The reward, on the other hand, was becoming a true partner in raising children and sharing the responsibility with someone else. My friend Judith put it this way:

The good thing for me about co-parenting is that I've learned that I'm not the only person who can care for the children and create love that sustains them. That, of course, is a big lesson, that whole letting-go process. And in the letting go, I have come to feel more free. I can feel really happy with the children now without feeling burdened by all the responsibilities, because Bill and I share them.

Perhaps you, father, remember being encouraged by your wife to diaper the baby. You were afraid to do it, didn't think you could deal with that job, but thought probably you should try. You did it, fumbled around some, accomplished the task, and in the process actually had fun with your baby. But wait, mother. He didn't do it right. The diaper pin isn't on tight enough; it looks like a pretty sloppy job to you. Can you let it be? Can you let him do it his way? It was clear that if father was going to be involved with the baby he would do it his way, which in all probability would not be your way. Could you trust this man with your baby?

Greater involvement on the part of men allowed women some child-free time within their marriage—the chance to go back to school, pursue career goals, and in general be something other than wife and mother. Participation by fathers also allowed women to feel that they were supported, both physically and emotionally, in the demanding job of child rearing. When marriages in which there was some shared responsibility dissolved, neither parent was willing to assume the role of the non-custodial parent. Some fathers, as well as mothers, wanted full custody of their children and agreed to co-parenting as a way to avoid major court battles. As one man told me, "The reason I want to be a half-time parent and do co-parenting is because I want to be a full-time parent. And I realize that

Marcia, my ex-wife, feels the same way and that our daughter wants the best of each of us."

Co-parenting evolved, therefore, out of the desire of both parents to continue being actively involved and their unwillingness to view separation or divorce as equivalent to one parent abandoning or "losing" the children.

Since I take co-parenting for granted, it's always puzzling to me when people have a traditional custody arrangement. And the reason I take it for granted is that it seems like a logical extension of the kind of relationship that Ian and I have always had with our child. When we decided to have a child, our intention was that Ian would be as involved a parent as I, and that's always been the case. I can't imagine living my life in any other way, in terms of the participation I would want from my child's father. The traditional role division in intact families is fairly destructive where the man is the breadwinner and spends significantly less time with his children; the woman has major responsibility for that and ends up feeling a lot of guilt because she has to meet impossibly high expectations as an active parent. So I guess that the whole system as we know it is pretty mixed up. For myself, anyway, I never wanted to live that way when I was married, and I certainly don't want to have to move toward that now that I'm not living with my child's father. Co-parenting meets my needs to be an active parent to my daughter, and to have time for myself. [Carolyn]

Is co-parenting for you? Is it a system you want to consider? There are many things to think about.

Do you feel you want to spend a fair amount of time working out arrangements with the person you just separated from? You should know that while you may talk to your ex-spouse almost every day in the beginning of a separation, that will wind down as your routine gets more stabilized, and your phone calls might get down to one or two a week.

Do you feel comfortable doing something that is seen as unconventional? You will not get a lot of support for co-parenting unless you seek out like-minded souls who have similar values and experiences. What you will get is gratuitous advice that you will not appreciate. Just expect to run into opposition about your decision to co-parent, and go on from there.

In a recent conversation with Dee, Joshua's after-school sitter, I asked about her thoughts on co-parenting. She said:

At first, co-parenting sounded dumb to me, I'll be honest with you. I had never heard of it before, I think that's what it was. But within the past year I've seen it really works out well for Joshua. He gets to see you both, gets a chance to do more. He has two people to answer to, just like in a regular family. And he's not a confused child at all. Just the opposite. He knows more what's going on than you, me and Jeff. So I feel differently about co-parenting now that I've seen the system work.

During the last few months, several couples have approached Jeff and me to spend an evening talking with them about co-parenting. They heard about us, wanted to learn how our system works for us, and wanted to get help thinking about their own needs. These discussions make sense. It is important to find people who can be supportive of you. Ask your friends if they know anybody who is co-parenting. Call that person up and ask if you can talk for a while. It's fine if the person you call is a stranger to you. Chances are he or she will be more than willing to share experiences and will be pleased to know another couple who may decide to co-parent. People who co-parent often feel that they are doing something unusual, maybe even a little crazy, that they are in it alone, and that they are going against the tide of popular opinion as to what's in the best interests of the child.

I would also encourage each of you to find support groups for parents who are separated or divorced, groups where you would meet people in similar life situations. While you may be the only person in the group who is co-parenting, many of the feelings you are experiencing will be shared by others in the group. It is a great relief to know that you are not the only one feeling isolated or overwhelmed by your new responsibilities. Some places to begin looking for such groups are a YMCA or YMHA, a chapter of Parents Without Partners, or a local college which has a women's center. If you have the energy, put your own ad in your community newspaper and start your own group. Whatever you do, participate with others around your experiences.

Getting good support and working out the details of a new living arrangement require a special effort and good will on the part of both parents. If you are willing to make that effort, co-parenting can be a positive force in your family's life together.

How To Do It: Scheduling, Toys, Clothes, and Money

We've managed to work out all the details to make co-parenting work. It took us a while, but we've finally got it pretty much down to a routine now, and we just do the same arranging that any parents do. The difference, though, is that Jane doesn't do it all. From clothes shopping to school stuff and dentist appointments, we share it all, right down the line.

Warren Kane

How do you decide on a schedule? Should you give your children a voice in determining their living arrangements? How do you establish a new kind of relationship with your children? Do you have to live near your ex-spouse in order to successfully co-parent? What do you do about toys and clothes? How do you work out your financial arrangements? Who takes care of a sick child? Who will your children be with during vacations, holidays and birthdays? These questions and other points about establishing the mechanics of co-parenting will be covered in this chapter.

Whenever I used to hear about a co-parenting schedule that was different from the one that Jeff and I used, I almost automatically judged it wrong. I decided it wouldn't work for

31

any number of reasons. Either the children stayed at one house for too short a time, or too long a time, or the schedule didn't seem like a schedule at all, but more of a haphazard arrangement. Or the parents lived too far away from each other, such as in different parts of the city. I thought some parents were asking unreasonable things of their children. A child's life would be totally scattered by a particular schedule, I thought, or it would uproot a child terribly to have a certain kind of arrangement.

When I heard about co-parenting arrangements where parents lived hundreds of miles apart, I didn't understand that at all. About the time I started learning about children who lived for six months on the East coast and six months on the West, or a year in Ireland and then a year in New York, I was forced to rethink my position. All kinds of arrangements were, in fact, working. I realized that I had been judging any system that was different from mine in the same way that other people were judging me and mine. It was unknown, it wasn't created by me, no one asked for my permission to do it that way, and therefore it was wrong, and certainly harmful to the child.

What I see now is that any plan works if you want it to. By *works* I mean that both parents and the child are relatively happy and comfortable with the routine that has been established, and that the child is no more problem prone than any other child, no matter what the family's life style is.

You and your spouse are about to separate. You each want to maintain a close relationship with your children and decide to co-parent. Neither parent wants to let go; neither wants to be without the children for any long period of time. It can be very helpful at a time like this to get some outside help. This help need not be therapy and the person you turn to for help need not be a mental health professional. Someone whom both of you know and trust, someone who could listen to you both and help you sort out the issues would be the kind of person to turn to. The person you choose to help you at this time should be someone who you feel would support the basic idea of co-parenting and not work to convince you to try another system altogether.

The day before Jeff and I separated, we sat down with our friend Paula to talk about what the following week would bring. We were both too upset about the upheaval in our lives to think very clearly, and Paula forced us to focus on some practical matters that we hadn't been able to face ourselves. Paula suggested that we have a definite schedule worked out for Joshua's living arrangements before we actually separated. We agreed that we needed to have a clear sense of when we would each be with Joshua, and we definitely needed to tell him when he would be with each of us.

It is important to have a definite schedule as soon as possible, even though it may change with time.

According to our first schedule, which we followed for about a month, Joshua switched from one house to the other almost every other night. Looking back over that time, I see that this routine was set up with our needs in mind, not his. Joshua was a focal point in each of our lives—we each needed his physical presence for self-definition. Within a very short period of time, however, this plan proved unworkable. There was no continuity in our lives; what did exist was a great deal of confusion. No sooner had I gotten used to being with Joshua, and he with me, than he was off again. We were both in a constant state of agitation and had no time to ease in to any kind of routine with each other. Joshua chose to express his anger at me, not at Jeff, and so our times together were mostly unhappy times. Joshua was four at the time and had trouble keeping things straight in his mind. One day he said, "Where did I wake up this morning?" It was time for a change.

We then began to lengthen the continuous time Joshua spent with each of us. Within about three months after our separation, Jeff and I agreed to an arrangement which we are still following, almost four years later.

Joshua is with me from Sunday morning through Thursday morning. After school on Thursday, he goes to his sitter's house, where Jeff picks him up. He is with Jeff from Thursday afternoon until Sunday morning. Since Jeff and I live near each other, Joshua can easily go to the same school from either house. His neighborhood friends are the same and he has a sense of continuity from one parent's home to the other's. A graphic representation of our weekly schedule looks like this:

	MON.	TUES.	WED.	THURS.	FRI.	SAT.	SUN.
EVERY WEEK	X	X	X	X／Y	Y	Y	Y／X

X and Y each represent days spent at different homes.

Other plans I know about include:

(1) A situation in which the children never leave their home. For six months of the year, the mother lives with the children in the family home. For the following six months, the mother moves to an apartment that she and her ex-husband share, and he moves into the home. These parents do not want to disrupt their children's lives in any way and choose instead to be the ones to move back and forth. They visit regularly with the children when they are not the parent with primary responsibility.

(2) A schedule based on a two-week time period:

    Week one: Mon., Tues. — child with mother.

             Wed., Thurs. — child with father.

             Fri., Sat., Sun. — child with father.

    Week two: Mon., Tues. — child with mother.

             Wed., Thurs. — child with father.

             Fri., Sat., Sun. — child with mother.

In this arrangement, Mondays and Tuesdays are always the child's days to be with the mother, Wednesdays and Thursdays are always days to be with the father, and then the Friday-Saturday-Sunday period alternates every week. In this way, over a two-week period each parent has a full weekend child-free, and each parent has a long stretch of time to be with the child. The schedule gets charted as follows:

	MON.	TUES.	WED.	THURS.	FRI.	SAT.	SUN.
WEEK I	X	X	Y	Y	Y	Y	Y
WEEK II	X	X	Y	Y	X	X	X
WEEK III	X	X	Y	Y	Y	Y	Y
WEEK IV	X	X	Y	Y	X	X	X

X and Y each represent days spent at different homes.

(3) Division into six-month periods, with the child living with one parent for six months and then the other parent for the following six months.

(4) Same as the six-month plan, only on a yearly basis. A 13-year-old I know of had been alternating between living in Ireland for a year, and then in the States for the next year; he had been doing this for over six years, changing schools, culture, routines. His parents have now decided that he will stay in the United States for all his high school years.

(5) A schedule based on a four-week period, where two weeks are spent with the father, and then two weeks with the mother. As the chart shows, the weekend in the middle of the two-week period is spent with the other parent.

	MON.	TUES.	WED.	THURS.	FRI.	SAT.	SUN.
WEEK I	Y	Y	Y	Y	Y	X	X
WEEK II	Y	Y	Y	Y	Y	Y	Y
WEEK III	X	X	X	X	X	Y	Y
WEEK IV	X	X	X	X	X	X	X

X and Y each represent days spent at different homes.

(6) One week at mother's house, one week at father's house.

These are just some possibilities. In figuring out what would make sense for you, you can consider several broad areas: the ages of your children, the children's wishes, your work schedule and other time commitments, and geographical factors. Often, parents experiment with a variety of schedules before finding one which works well for everyone.

We've been separated for four years. The first two years I stayed in the house and John moved out and lived nearby. He would come and stay with the children on weekends and usually one afternoon during the week. When he was there, I would leave and stay with friends. Then the next year we reversed that arrangement and he stayed in the house and I lived with a group of people and just came and stayed with the children two-and-a-half to three days a week. And when I would come, he would leave. Then last fall, after the year he was in the house, we went through a very difficult time. We had an agreement that we would each live with the children in the house for half the week, and the other half we would live in an apartment we rented nearby. We didn't want the children to have to move back and forth, and thought it would be easier if we did. Well, for a lot of reasons this didn't work out. What happened was that we both ended up living in the house, in separate bedrooms, for three months, until we negotiated a new agreement. And we had to go to a counselor to do it.

What we finally worked out was that I would get my own separate apartment, which John would help me finance, and this is the first year that the children have moved back and forth between our two homes. Before this arrangement, one parent was in the house with the children, while the other parent was around enough so that we were definitely both part of their lives. Now, the children really have the same amount of time with each of us. Our schedule is that I have the children Wednesday afternoon through Saturday evening, and John has them Saturday night through Wednesday mornings. We pretty much stick to that, and it has taken us four years to work it out. [Jerilyn]

How many children do you have? Do you want all your children to be with you at the same time? Do you want some time when you can be with one child, instead of always being with all three? Parents need to consider such questions when deciding on a schedule.

Parents who have more than one child have reported that co-parenting allows them the time to be with each child separately and to develop a separate, special relationship with each child in a way that had not been possible previously.

We call it private time. There had always been competition between the kids for my attention. The marvelous bonus of co-parenting has allowed me to be with one child at a time and to really see and experience them as individual people, not as "the kids." [Joan]

Co-parenting allows for flexibility in schedules, much as is necessary for parents and children to experience togetherness and separateness. Some parents choose for all three children to go back and forth between houses at the same time. Others may want some private time with each child and will build that in to their schedule.

Our schedule is that the children spend two weeks with their father and two weeks with me. On the transition weekend, Michael makes the switch on Friday night and Rebecca stays until Sunday night. That way we each get to spend one weekend a month with one child. [Lois]

Some parents do not set aside time specifically to be with each child, but find that there is time to be with them separately. Jerilyn says, "It just works out that I spend time with Adam especially, because he is home from school before Zachary is. So we'll have a fair amount of time when it's just Adam and me. Since Adam goes to bed before Zachary, it usually works out that Zachary and I then do his homework together, or read together. I do get to be with them as individual children and I like that."

Most parents I know have not asked their young children what their preferences for living arrangements would be. To have to choose which parent to live with, and when, would put a great pressure on a young person. The older the child is, however, the more he or she will want to have a say about everything, including living arrangements. Do you want to give your child a voice in determining where he or she will live, and on which days? If his preference turns out not to be your preference, would you be willing to go along with that?

If I saw that Zachary needed to have that role model of being with John all the time, and that he had the kind of relationship with his father that did more for him than what I can give him, I really feel that I would agree to his being with John. That wouldn't be easy, but part of the problem is that there's four-and-a-half years' difference between Zachary and Adam. I can see that when Zachary gets to be twelve, thirteen, or fourteen, if he really wanted to be with John more I would let him make that choice and respect it. But I wouldn't want to split Adam and Zachary. They really do support each other and give each other a sense of continuity. It would be very very hard for me to give up Adam when he's still a little kid. And he's certainly not to the point where he could make that decision.[Jerilyn]

Children voice their preferences without our asking them. Jeff and I did not ask Joshua, who was four years old at the time, what his preferences were when we worked out our arrangement. We felt that he was too young to make that kind of decision and we did not want to put him in the position of having to choose. As he gets older, however, he may very well want to choose.

One boy I know lived in a co-parenting situation from the time he was five years old until he was twelve. Then, his father and his father's new wife decided to move to another state and the boy, Chris, decided he wanted to go with them. It was an extremely difficult situation for Lynn, his mother. She felt great pain and loss at the realization that she would not have a daily relationship with her son. She also wanted to respect her son's decision and agreed to his move.

Jan told the following story of her son's decision to live with his father:

At one point my child said that he felt like a yo-yo switching back from one week to the next week, so we started to do it month by month. We each wanted that continuity, going through school days and weekends; at the end of the month it was like a huge caravan that would move from one house to the other. And then he said he still felt like a yo-yo and had difficulty with parting; finally he told me this spring, age 10, "You know mom, when I was littler, I needed you, you were my mommy, and I didn't know daddy well." He said, "Well, I'm 10 now and I'm a boy and I want to grow up to be a man like my father. I don't want this to hurt your feelings, but can I live with my father? I need to stay in one place." I was really so glad he could say that and told him we would work it out. The need for one place and one neighborhood was great. He bicycles over to see me every afternoon, so it isn't like a real separation.

There are times such as these when we need to give our children permission to have lives of their own, separate from ours.

What are your time commitments? In planning your schedule, you should keep in mind what your work schedules will be, how much time you will have available to really be with your children on your "on" days, and what your own needs for free time are. Jeff and I came to our particular schedule after seeing that he often had evening meetings during the week, whereas my week nights were usually free. Jeff wanted to have Joshua with him all weekend, but I wanted to be with Joshua on Sunday, when we could visit friends, go to a movie, or generally spend relaxing times together.

Be flexible about changing your schedule over time. What works at any given time in our lives may no longer be feasible at another time. The schedule that we make when we first separate may become less desirable a few years later.

It's part of our written separation agreement that we will negotiate the schedule each year. Part of that negotiation involves surveying what the two children want. Both Marvin and I feel it's very important to keep listening to the kids, to hear their needs. They're 10 and 13 now, and their needs will change and we both feel we want to be open to change to meet their needs. So that's why we wrote it in our agreement. And we read that part of the agreement to the kids, so that they'd know we were very serious about listening to them.[Lois]

At one point, Jeff and I had considered changing our schedule so that Joshua would be with one of us for a full week and then with the other for a full week. This plan appeals to me; for now, on occasions when Joshua is with me for a longer stretch of time than usual, we often get into a finer rhythm of being together. We are able to do a greater variety of things together. (According to our present schedule, for instance, I never have Joshua for a full weekend; so if I want to go away with him, I have to make special arrangements with Jeff.) Though contemplating changes in routine is anxiety-producing for us, we are still always open to considering change. Jeff and I both realize that our present plan is not one we have to adhere to forever; things *do* change. Those of us who are separated or divorced certainly know that nothing, or not much anyway, is forever.

Explain the schedule to your children in a clear, straightforward way. Using charts, like the ones presented earlier in this chapter, will be helpful.

You have probably told your children that you are separating, and now you need to give them a clear picture of what the new living arrangements will be. Children need to have a sense of predictability, to know what is happening, when and where. A two year old will not grasp the full meaning of your separation and its consequences, but should be told in much the same way you would tell an older child. The clearer we can be about schedules the easier it will be for children to understand that relationships with both parents will be continual.

Parents should present the co-parenting plan to their child together.

A child will immediately sense that there is some degree of cooperation between his parents and realize that, even though they may be angry at each other, they both can put problems aside and remain loving, involved people in his life. You can tell your child that it might take some time for all of you to get used to new living arrangements and that you will cooperate with each other to make your system work. Your child should know that you and your ex-spouse will be in touch with each other frequently and will continue to plan together to meet his needs.

Should you and your ex-spouse live close to each other?

When Jeff and I first talked about separating and who would move out, we felt that the only way our co-parenting system would work was if we lived close to one another. We both wanted to be involved in Joshua's daily routine of catching the school bus, picking him up at his usual after-school sitter's, being close to his friends and familiar neighborhood activities. Much less of this would be possible if we lived some distance apart. We felt it was important for there to be continuity in Joshua's life, and we saw geographical proximity as a key element in making this happen. Jeff eventually got an apartment a few minutes away from mine so that Joshua hasn't had to shift gears totally when he moves from one house to the other.

This arrangement has its disadvantages. Do you want to see your ex-spouse in the supermarket? Do you feel comfortable with the idea that you might run into your ex-spouse and his lover at your friendly neighborhood movie theatre? The local shopkeepers assume you are still married since you both still frequent the same stores, and the pharmacist doesn't quite understand why you need two bottles of cough medicine instead of one. The psychological factor of knowing your ex-spouse lives nearby can be either a positive or a negative experience for you, or both. On the one hand, there is the comfort of knowing that you can get help in an emergency; on the other, the process of separating emotionally seems that much more difficult, knowing that you still live practically within earshot of your former spouse.

What living arrangements would best suit your needs?

Perhaps the neighborhood where you've been living as an intact family is not suited for single parenthood. The suburban life may seem stifling, now that you've separated; and as much as you want to co-parent, you feel that living in your old neighborhood would be very unsatisfying for you. There are several alternatives to think about. One would be the possibility of staying in the same locale for a year or so, and view this as a period of adjustment during which you and your child would be able to get used to a new way of living. You would be able to maintain close contact with your child and you could spend some of your child-free time discovering different parts of the city where you might want to live some time in the future. If you decide to remain in the same geographical area for now, that doesn't mean it will be forever. It means that for right now you have chosen to live close to your ex-spouse in order to work out an easier system of co-parenting.

Another possibility is that you would decide to move away from your original neighborhood. You would probably have to do some extra driving to get your child to school and to arrange for visits with his playmates. These visits will probably become less necessary over time, as your child forms friendships in your new living situation.

It is possible to work out creative solutions to the problem of geographical distance. Some people know for sure that they want to live far away from their ex-spouse. They also know that they want to maintain an intimate relationship with their children. What's important for all of us to remember who are involved in raising children after a separation is that this is not the way we planned it, none of us. Most of us assumed that we would continue to be married and raise our children, perhaps according to some personal fantasy of American family life. But that is not how it turned out. To people looking from the outside, an arrangement where children alternate between living for one year in California with the mother and living the next year in New Hampshire with the father might seem emotionally destructive; yet to the parents and the children involved, it is the best possible solution to their unique situation, one in which there may be pains and one in which there definitely are pleasures.

Working out in advance other schedule-related matters — for example, illness, vacations, holidays, and birthdays — is an important part of establishing your new routine.

When Joshua gets sick on one of "my" days, I do not assume that I am responsible for taking care of him. By our agreement, I call Jeff and we figure out which one of us is more available than the other to be with Joshua that day. I am a social worker and Jeff is a teacher. If I have an important meeting scheduled at work, then I would ask Jeff to take over. If he has a class to teach at the same time as my meeting, we work out some compromise. Where I work Joshua can often come with me; as he gets older, this becomes easier to do since he can amuse himself for a good part of the day. Jeff and I do share the responsibility of caring for Joshua's health and medical needs, no matter what day any special problem happens to fall on.

Vacations need to be scheduled as much in advance as possible. If I know in March that I want to travel by myself for the last two weeks of August, I tell Jeff my plans, confirm that Joshua can be with him, and them consider that time to be mine. For holidays such as July 4th and Thanksgiving, we usually keep to our basic schedule. Occasionally we both want to spend some special time with Joshua, and usually we are able to accommodate each other's wishes. This year Joshua, Jeff, and I, along with some close friends, all celebrated Thanksgiving together.

We're still just working out holidays because we've been separated only a year. Ian has no parents, and last Christmas he was very encouraging for our five-year-old daughter Jessie to be with me and my family. He's very giving in that way. He likes the fact that our daughter has grandparents. Now it's Ian's year to have Jessie at Christmas. But Sara, the woman he lives with, is on an alternate year holiday schedule with her child, and he wants to regularize that with her. However, this Christmas my family and I are going to take a family vacation, probably without Jessie. So I said that she could be with him this Christmas and the next one too if he needed to get his schedule aligned with Sara's. Now, maybe come next Christmas I might not feel so magnanimous about that. It might be really painful for me not to have Jessie around on Christmas. But I guess because I have my family I could go to them and get a lot of support from them. They make holidays for me. If Jessie is there, that's a big plus; and if she isn't, I can cope with it.[Carolyn]

Birthdays are easy to manage. Most co-parents I know alternate years in which they are responsible for the child's birthday party. One year Jeff organized things at his house, I baked the cake, and we shared the costs. Another year, we took several children out to a puppet show and shared that expense. We also alternate baking the brownies for Joshua's party at school. Usually Jeff and I coordinate plans for buying Joshua's birthday presents.

How To Do It: Scheduling, Toys, Clothes, and Money

How do you decide which toys go to which residence?

Children usually have a supply of toys at each parent's home, some of which may go back and forth between the two places. Occasionally it happens that Joshua will be at my house and be very upset when he realizes that he wants to play with a certain toy that he left at his father's house. My reaction to this situation is mixed. In the past I have felt sorry that he had to live this way — with his possessions scattered to the wind (that's the feeling, although it's only two places) — and felt that I should make every effort to get that toy. That would usually mean a phone call to Jeff and, if he was home, a ride over there. Now, this doesn't take much time, but the feeling is that I'd rather not be involved. I want Joshua to take responsibility for knowing where his things are and what he's going to want at which house. That may be a tall order for a child. I know that he does need to take charge of this aspect of his life and not see himself as a victim of circumstances. Sometimes I get the toy from Jeff's, and sometimes I don't. My intention is not to be rigid, but to understand the importance of the situation to Joshua at the moment.

One toy that routinely travels between our houses is Joshua's bike. This can only be described as an annoyance—yet important enough to Joshua for us to continue transporting it. In a few years Joshua will be old enough to ride his bike from one house to another, which will eliminate the annoyance, give Joshua a greater sense of independence, and probably create other problems. For now, however, Jeff and I are aware of which items of Joshua's need to go back and forth with him.

Our agreement is that if the kids leave something at my apartment and want it at their father's, it's my responsibility to get it there. The same holds true for him. If they leave something at their father's apartment and find they want it when they're at my place, he has to get it here. This has cut down considerably on things being left behind inadvertently. Before they leave here, I go over with them very carefully if they've got everything they're going to need for the next two weeks. I know I don't want to be making extra trips across town, bringing them a book report or a pair of sneakers.[Lois]

45

One way to involve your child in the decision-making process is to ask him which toys he would like to have at mother's and which at father's. To most children this is important. A four year old associates certain toys with one parent or the other. Joshua knows that I don't like board games and I do like jigsaw puzzles, so if he wants me for a playmate, it behooves him to have his jigsaw puzzles at my house. Of course, leaving the whole job of dividing up toys may be overwhelming to a child; but there definitely is room for his involvement in this area.

Children usually have a set of clothes in each home. When Jeff and I first started co-parenting, I was very conscious of which clothes Joshua wore on the day that he went to his father's house. I helped him select his older, more worn out clothes. I knew that possibly I wouldn't see these clothes for a long time, and I would rather have the nicer clothes in my house than in Jeff's house. My excuse for that behavior was that I thought Jeff was fairly unconscious about what Joshua was wearing. As it turns out, he knew all along what I was up to, and for a time tacitly agreed with this system. In time, things began to change.

I used to do all the clothes buying. Initially we agreed that Jeff would be responsible for Joshua's medical attention (checkups, the dentist, vitamin re-fills), and I would take care of the clothes. I wanted it this way because I didn't trust Jeff's taste in clothes. After almost three years, I got tired of this system and Jeff wanted to do some of the clothes buying. This was an area in which I had to give up some control if I wanted Jeff to share in the responsibility. He might pick out clothes for Joshua that I thought were less attractive, but he would be picking out the clothes at least some of the time, and that became more important to me. Jeff's taste has improved over the years, by my standards anyway. And now Joshua is choosing his own clothes with guidance.

I now see clothes on Joshua that I have had no part in choosing. I have no idea where they were bought, how long he's had them, if his other Grandma gave them to him, or what. Sometimes it gives me a strange feeling to know that there is a big part of his life that doesn't include me at all. Clothes are just a symbol of this to me, since Joshua has many experiences that I am totally unaware of. Of course, not all parents in intact families know everything their child has done or is doing; but when I see Joshua wearing a T-shirt that I've never seen before, it reminds me that a lot of his life is very separate from mine. Sometimes that feels fine with me, and sometimes it feels strange.

My friend Carolyn reports that she and Ian each take responsibility for buying clothes for Jessie at their separate apartments. Says Carolyn,

I know some couples who get into fighting about what dress got left where. We're very respectful of each other about that. If it ends up that some things which Ian bought Jessie are at my house, at the end of a month I'll make up a bag and send that back over.

Lois, who has two children, says that she shops for two wardrobes for her daughter and her ex-husband takes care of two wardrobes for their son.

Kathy and her brother Robbie live with their mother for two weeks and then their father for two weeks. They do not have sets of clothing at each house.

We just pack up all our clothes, get these big suitcases, and walk over there. People think we're running from home and it gets embarrassing because we have to go right past the bus stop.[Kathy, age 13]

Invariably, after the first snowfall, the child's boots will be at the other parent's house and a frantic call will be made early in the morning to arrange for a boots transfer. In my experience, even if the child has two pairs of boots, they both usually wind up in one house and there are no boots in the house where the child needs them. It's a small thing, yet it tells me that Jeff and I can plan all we want, can see to it that we've covered all the bases, so to speak, and yet we can always be caught short. No matter how much in control of the situation we think we are, sometimes we're just not.

When we first separated, I used to get back Joshua's clothes that needed mending. I got ripped pants to repair, to sew a patch on, an armhole that needed a reinforced seam. I don't know exactly how this changed, but I realized that this had stopped and Jeff was beginning to do the repair jobs that came his way. It felt to me that he was saying that he wanted to be responsible for all areas of Joshua's life that he was involved in, and that included areas that we both previously assumed I would be in charge of. (I was reluctant to assume responsibility for areas in which I felt Jeff was more competent. If Joshua wanted to build something, I'd suggest he do it with Jeff. There's nothing wrong with recognizing our own strengths and weaknesses, but I know full well how to bang a nail into a piece of wood and how to use a saw. I just wasn't willing to work harder at things that didn't come easy for me.)

Settle your financial agreement as soon as possible.

Money matters, and how to work them out, seem to absorb a great deal of time and emotional investment right after a separation takes place. It is difficult to establish what is "fair," how to compensate for a woman's job of working inside the home and not having any income or credit rating of her own, how to figure out which expenses are the child's, and what might be considered the mother's. At best it is a complicated business. I want to describe to you the financial arrangement that Jeff and I have worked out, with the full realization that it would not work for everyone.

We each keep track of what our Joshua-related expenses are within a period of a month. If I buy socks for Joshua, I write down the cost. If I pay a doctor bill, I keep track of the cost. Jeff and I have agreed on certain areas in which we share costs for Joshua, and these are listed in our separation agreement (shown in Chapter 5). At the end of the month, we tell each other what our expenses have been and figure out whether Jeff owes me money or I owe him money, based on who spent what during the month. We have agreed to share financial responsibility on a pro-rated basis according to our incomes. At this point, Jeff pays 57% of Joshua's costs and I pay 43%. So, we compare our separate expenses for the month and work out the percentage of our costs. The actual money involved seems minimal. It feels right to me that we share in Joshua's costs in direct proportion to our incomes. One month I may buy Joshua a winter coat and would need Jeff's share in order to pay the bill, so I like working it out on a month-to-month basis. Many people think that our system is unwieldy and that they would be unable to keep track of expenses in the detail that we do. It has been working well for us.

Here are some examples of how other co-parents have worked out their financial arrangements:

We have the same income, so we split monies evenly. We account for all our finances quarterly. If there was a bill that was more than $200, we pay that up right away. [Lois]

Doctor bills, clothes, anything that either of us has to get for Jonathan, we know what our respective incomes are and what our proportionate share is. So if I get a pair of shoes, I'll call Ann and say, "Well, I got the shoes." Jonathan knows that whatever it is, it's shared. [Bruce]

I give Marilynn $20 a week for food and things like that and I think she spends a lot more when Rachael is with her. I guarantee all of Rachael's clothes, school, camp, medical bills, and other things that come up. When Marilynn gets into a position of greater earning capacity, she'll contribute a greater portion. I think that it pains Marilynn that she can't do that. So she makes a direct and very, very strong effort to take on other areas of Rachael's care: logistical areas. It's easier for her to do the logistics, it's easier for me to do the money. [Larry]

Sally and I never exchange any money. I would give her money if she asked for it. I've loaned her money personally, but not for Aaron.

Only now we're having a little conflict. She wants to put money aside for Aaron's college, and I guess I could think of doing that. I guess I'll put some aside. But we never exchange money. This income tax year, she takes responsibility; next year, I take it. The insurance depends on who's covered. This year she happens to be covered through work.[Evan]

Financially I'm responsible for the children, even though that's not in our agreement. Bill is very irresponsible about getting his economics in order. It's written into the separation agreement that we'll both obviously take care of the children and provide for their financial needs when they're with us. However, all the medical expenses, all tuition expenses, clothes, etc.—I've done just about all that. I presented Bill with a list of expenses a couple months ago, and said this is what you owe me. He hit the ceiling, he was furious that I didn't trust him enough. I said, "Look, I trusted you for four years, and you haven't come through. Now I'm showing you what it costs to take care of children and to raise them. I expect you to hold your end up." This was a big problem when we were married and it's still a big problem today. I haven't seen any money yet.[Judith]

I don't look at it as money, where one does this much and the other does that much. Whatever we feel we have to do, we do. My income is much higher than Sheila's. We have a lot of trust between us now, so that she can call me up to say she needs some money. I don't feel benevolent about it either. It's just not important to me. There's a friendship and I'm doing it because she's a friend of mine, not because I feel obligated. We have a name for it: we call it friends who happen to be parents of the same children.[Charles]

One special consideration involving money arises when the mother takes a job which will allow her to be home with the children after school. It is likely a job which pays less money than one in which she would be working from nine o'clock to five. Her income will be considerably less than her ex-husband's. In this situation, a strict proportion of incomes should be adjusted to include the fact that the mother's ability to be home after school is saving in childcare costs. If this is a preferable arrangement for the children, then the amount of her financial contribution ought to be thoughtfully worked out.

John pays child support plus some to cover my expenses. The way we worked it out was that I would support myself and he would support the children and give me whatever was required to cover their part of my household. We went over the figures, almost penny by penny, what the expenses would be, and what his share of it would be. This apartment was the only thing I could find nearby with two bedrooms and decent enough to live in. The rent is more than I make per month, since I only work part time. So John agreed, in order for us to continue co-parenting, that he would cover as much of my rent that I couldn't. He gives me $377 a month and I feel like I can survive for a couple of years this way. Most of the time I feel I'm living at the poverty line, but it's worth it to me not to have to work full time now, while the children are still young. [Jerilyn]

Don't be afraid to leave your child with a sitter or otherwise experiment with the mechanics of your routine.

For almost a full two years after we separated, I did not make any other plans for the times I was scheduled to be with Joshua. When he was with me, I really wanted to be *with* him. I figured that I had three-and-a-half days a week for myself and I considered the time Joshua was with me as very precious. I would not accept dinner invitations to a friend's house, rarely went to a meeting if it was on an "on" night, and clearly saw my priority as being with Joshua. I was unwilling to leave him with a sitter, and felt that doing this met my own need to be totally available to Joshua whenever he was with me. Now, within the last year or so, I have made different kinds of choices about how I spend my time. I chose to take a course one semester on an evening when Joshua was with me, and I occasionally get a sitter and go out to a movie or a concert on a weeknight. I do think about what effect being out often would have on Joshua, and I am careful not to push either his limits or mine. And I still feel available to him.

Depending how comfortable you feel with the situation, you may want to accompany your children to your ex-spouse's home one time. A child can derive comfort from knowing that you see how and where he lives when he is not with you. This need not be an extensive visit, but enough to give your child a chance to show you his other home and let you see the things he has there.

As a means of helping your child ease into the day when he switches living quarters, you might want to regularize the plan of telephoning your child either the night before the switch or early in the morning of the switch day. This would give you a chance to check in, talk about plans for the next few days, discuss what special items your child might want to bring over to your house, and generally reestablish direct contact. It's a nice way to begin your days together.

The mechanics of co-parenting take some time to work out. However, once you have had practice in carrying out your particular arrangements, the system can operate smoothly.

As you both—mother and father—gradually take on all tasks related to child raising, you each have a feeling of increased competence, more confidence in yourself as a parent, and satisfaction from your continual interaction with your children.

I am often called by Joshua's school to bake something for the Spring Thing, or for a special bake sale. I don't particularly enjoy baking; Jeff does. I have learned to ask the person to call Jeff at his home—and while it used to feel weird to have to do this, it was better than committing myself to more chocolate chip cookies than I'd care to deal with. People are often very surprised about our arrangement, and then very impressed that we manage to achieve what was assumed to be impossible—consistent, loving care for a child from two parents who happen to be divorced.

Your Relationship
With Your Ex-Spouse

We have had to face up to a lot of stuff about our feelings for each other. We actually continue to have, in many ways, a more productive relationship now than we ever did when we were together, because we have gotten on a new ground together in terms of mutual respect, mutual recognition, and a lot of things that we never could do when we were married. Our relationship now is based on factors that support our being friends. It's kind of neat. I really have begun to appreciate John and trust him in ways that I never did before.

Jerilyn Ransom

Learning to maintain the parent system while you are dissolving the spouse system can be a delicate task. In order to co-parent effectively, you need to have a fairly close relationship with your ex-spouse. This may conflict directly with your emotional needs after a separation—especially, the need to create distance between one another. Yet it *is* possible to establish a relationship with your ex-spouse that contains such seeming contradictions.

People are often suspicious of any relationship you might have with the person you were once married to, not to mention a steady, cooperative one. My stereotyped view of what ex-spouses did with each other was that they spoke only when absolutely necessary. Anything other than that was clearly a neurotic need to stay close to someone you obviously shouldn't feel close to anymore.

If you're such good friends, people would say, and able to get along so well, then why did you divorce? The people who now divorce are no longer just those who are totally miserable with each other, but also those who may choose not to live together any more although they still like each other. Today, more ex-spouses are choosing to stay in touch with each other and define their relationship as it suits them, not necessarily as society dictates. This is particularly true for people who have children and who desire to remain active, loving parents. They understand that co-parenting requires a good working relationship between ex-spouses.

What is my basic attitude about working out custody and the whole situation of the family that's split up? Well, I feel it's important for people to take a measure of themselves and their situation, to work out something that really suits them and their needs, and not just follow some formula that is the given method of dealing with the situation according to somebody else's rules. Traditionally, people expect that as soon as you separate from your mate you cut off all relationships with that person and go out and start a new life. It's just a radical severing, no matter how much you've been involved with that person, even if you've been married to him twenty years. I think that that's very inhuman and unreal. You've certainly got some good things going with somebody whom you've spent that much of your life with—and certainly the children have ties that just can't be severed. You really need to work out something where the human heart can be kept intact. That's why I think co-parenting is a good option to consider, because it does allow you a great deal more flexibility. [Roberta]

How much contact should two people who used to be married have with each other? There are no rules. At times you will want to be talking a lot, at other times you will prefer to avoid having contact with one another. At first you will probably experience conflicting needs and emotions and live with opposing feelings. But whatever your relationship is now with your ex-spouse, it will change. Change is the nature of all relationships, especially one in which you have put a great deal of emotional energy. The relationship you have with your ex-spouse, particularly right after a separation takes place, is not a neutral one. It would be a rare couple who could separate one day and have a great deal of trust for each other the next day. Feelings of trust develop slowly after a separation, even though they may have existed during your marriage. You need time to pull back, to separate yourself from your ex-spouse, to work out your need to mourn the loss of this relationship. A period of withdrawal from your ex-spouse is natural after separating. It is natural in this period to deny that anything good ever existed in this relationship. Forging your new identity as a separate person sometimes comes in conflict with maintaining a civil relationship with your ex-spouse.

I have referred to the delicacy in a relationship between two people who are no longer married to each other but who are involved with each other through their commitment to co-parenting. The delicacy exists because it is difficult to give each other support as parents *and* at the same time withdraw from each other's emotional lives. It is easy to fall back to the patterns that used to be destructive in your relationship, the ones that brought you no pleasure and much guilt, or hurt, or whatever it was that didn't feel good. You will get angry at each other in the same way you used to, and you will feel loving toward each other in the same way you used to. It takes time to break habits and for you to establish new patterns of interacting. For this is what your relationship with your ex-spouse is about now—building on what was good and decent in your past relationship while creating new forms of communicating as you co-parent.

The hardest part of co-parenting for me has been setting the limits of our friendship—because Marcia and I don't want it to move back to the areas that were difficult for us in the past. And yet we have to maintain a closeness necessary for child rearing, at least as we've defined it. No matter where we are in our relationship with each other, if something comes up, we have to call each other and communicate about it. There could be important areas of our daughter's growth that might otherwise get ignored. We can't let other elements of our relationship interfere with talking about why she hates math, what's happening with her friends, and so on.[Steve]

Even if you are not feeling good about your ex-spouse you can still co-parent. You can cooperate with each other enough to establish schedules, work out financial arrangements, and arrange for the details of child-caring. You can be angry as hell at one another and still co-parent.

Our values are completely different, which is one of the reasons why we broke up. The latest conversation I had with my ex-husband was the first one in maybe a year. That's how much we communicate. We don't communicate at all; we are ships in the night. We don't have to talk, though. We're not fighting; but, on the other hand, there's nothing really positive either, except that I always respected Bob's relationship with the children, and he knows that.[Jennifer]

Your relationship with your ex-spouse, then, is unique for the two of you. What might work for one couple would be disaster for another. In time, the two of you will find your own delicate balance.

How do you begin then to create an effective co-parenting relationship with your ex-spouse?

It may be very confusing, especially at first, to figure out how many and what kind of discussions you need to have with each other in order to co-parent. Limiting your initial discussions to business items—like arranging the mechanics of co-parenting—might be helpful at first. One of the things you may need to do is make new day-care arrangements for your child. Doing this would give you the opportunity to work with each other on a specific task. You could interview sitters together or visit your child's school for a discussion with his teacher(s). The focus of the time you spend with each other now is on planning together for your child's needs.

When Jeff and I first separated, there was a great deal of anger and bitterness between us. We were fairly suspicious of each other, and although we wanted (intellectually) to be on good terms, we didn't trust each other much at all. Separation was painful; the task of rebuilding our separate lives occupied much of our emotional lives. During this initial period of separation, though, we talked on the phone almost daily. The reason we gave ourselves then for this constant interaction was that we needed to work out arrangements for Joshua. That may have been so. I see now that we also needed to stay in close contact with each other to meet our own needs.

Jeff and I felt it was important to share the reactions that Joshua was having to our separation and the ways we each responded to those reactions.

At the time, Joshua's anger was expressed mostly with me and toward me. As much as Jeff and I talked about this, I felt unsupported by Jeff and angry at him for not receiving any of Joshua's disruptive behavior. Joshua was upset when he was with me, and I wanted Jeff to experience this upset as well. Joshua knew how unhappy I was then, and I guess I allowed and encouraged him to be unhappy. But Jeff was in pretty good shape psychologically, and I think Joshua responded to this by feeling better himself when he was with Jeff. It seemed as if there was nothing else to do but talk about the situation, try to deal with it, figure out strategies for helping Joshua. Jeff and I were always talking on the phone. Occasionally we would also meet in some neutral territory, such as a friend's house or a local coffee shop, to talk some more.

While many of these early meetings centered on working out financial matters, beyond that they gave us an opportunity just to see each other. We wanted to retain *some* contact—and I suppose the amount of contact we had was exactly what we needed. At times when it seemed like too much, one of us would slow things down by suggesting that we not meet for a week or that we talk less often on the phone. Now, Jeff and I talk to each other often, several times a week, although in much less depth than previously. We talk mostly about arrangements, schedules, quick questions. Periodically we get together to discuss whatever issues may have come up concerning Joshua, to talk about his schooling, and in general to exchange views about how we see him getting along in life. While these meetings usually have some agenda, we use them more as a free flowing time and see what emerges for each of us.

We have also used such an occasion to review our own relationship. We have shared insights about what went on in our marriage, and about how we now see what our behavior meant then. We have continued to use our present relationship to understand what happened and happens between us; from this, we see ourselves better in relation to our separate worlds. What we have learned over the past few years is that we can feel good about each other as people and as parents to Joshua. We acknowledge that we have a continuing relationship with each other. We don't have to deny the good things that existed in our married relationship—we build on those things. Basically, throughout most of the time we've known each other, Jeff and I have been able to be good friends to one another. This has enabled us to be good parents to Joshua in that we can talk about what is going on with him and with us. Our past relationship now exists in its present form to serve co-parenting. It is by no means *the* model relationship which needs to exist in order to make co-parenting work.

My friends Carolyn and Ian are co-parents who have another kind of relationship.

Ian is very good with young children. He likes to play and he's really good at playing and being silly. I'm not. For a couple of years I was feeling inadequate in relation to that, and feeling that I should be more that way. Then I decided no—I am who I am and I can be a parent in the way that I know, in the way that feels comfortable to me. This summer I've had to be away from Jessie quite a bit because of vacations and because of work that I do. When she started getting very clutchy with me, I told Ian that I was having a hard time with her. I said that I was really needing to spend less time with Jessie and that it was a big strain on me as a single parent. I wanted Ian to have her more days a week than our usual schedule and I wanted to be able to talk to him about my feelings. He got very threatened and did not want to talk about those things—or when we did, I felt that he was judgmental of me and basically was saying I was not a good parent. I have come to realize that I was taking in his judgments of me as a bad parent and letting that shake me and determine how I felt about myself. And I don't need to do that. I'm the one who can decide and evaluate for myself what kind of parent I am. And though we do talk to each other about some basic things that we need to in relation to Jessie, I've come to see that I'm not going to get the kind of support from him that I see other co-parenting couples have. [Carolyn]

Jeff and I usually talk on the phone the night before Joshua changes houses. We use this opportunity to talk about what Joshua's days have been like, what kind of mood he's been in, and if anything special has happened. One of the nicest things Jeff and I do for each other is report back Joshua's cute remarks or interesting thoughts—the kind that no one appreciates as much as we do. Barbara, Jeff's girlfriend, says that she really sees the enjoyment Jeff and I get out of sharing stories about Joshua. "There is no one quite like a parent to get in there and see how wonderful and special this light of the earth is. I see you and Jeff get that from each other." It is because we realize that we both miss out on some important times by not being with Joshua more that we keep each other informed of those things which only a parent cares about. I believe, however, that co-parenting can work effectively without this kind of exchange between parents. You can be a loving parent to a child and assume your share of responsibility without knowing what your child's days have been like with the other parent. There were times when I didn't really want to know how easy a time Jeff had with Joshua, because his days with me were not too happy. There is no right way or wrong way to communicate with your ex-spouse when you are involved in co-parenting. The only thing that makes something right or wrong is how it feels to you.

Co-Parenting

Whatever kind of relationship you work out with your ex-spouse, your purpose now is to continue sharing the responsibilities for bringing up your children. You will always be related to each other through your children and that bond will exist between you no matter how you choose to use it. Jeff and I have chosen to use that bond to strengthen our relationship as loving parents to Joshua. Yet that doesn't mean that all our views on parenting are the same. We do share similar values, by and large, but we do have our differences. Most people usually assume that, in order to co-parent successfully, parents must view life similarly and raise their children with similar values. Parents living in a nuclear family often have disagreements about child rearing; the children know it, but no one suggests they divorce or put their children up for adoption. Yet when parents who co-parent have differences, it is somehow seen as more serious and more disruptive to the children's emotional well-being. I don't think that's necessarily so. What is important here is how those differences are handled.

An issue may arise when one parent is easier on discipline than the other so that that parent's house is an easier place for the child to be. Haika pees at night, still, and one of the funnier discussions Marcia and I had was trying to discover where Haika pees more, her house or mine. It turned out for whatever reason to be Marcia's. Now, this bordered on a serious discussion when Marcia advocated using some machine that goes off when the child pees—it wakes up the whole block, everybody but the kid, everybody else would get up and pee. It's a water-sensitive pad that sets off a bell when it gets wet. I told Marcia I didn't want her to use such a horrendous device. She was a little angry because she already had sent for it and believed it would work. This could have become one of those issues that cause us to flare up for a while, but fortunately it wasn't. Finally I told Marcia I would do everything to support her using it at her house. As it turns out, she decided not to use it.[Steve]

There seems to be no need for Jeff and me to argue out the differences. Recently Jeff told me that he thought I was too lenient with Joshua around bedtime and that Joshua gets tired early when he gets to Jeff's house on Thursdays because he has gotten to bed late at my house on Wednesdays. Jeff wondered if this was because I thought Joshua didn't need that much sleep, or if I allowed him to stay up late because of my need for company. Previously, I would have gotten upset at what I would have taken as criticism of my parenting. I believe that Joshua can regulate himself around sleep and, yes, I do like his company. I also do tell him to get to bed when I think it's time. I didn't feel I had to do it Jeff's way, or argue about the "right way" to do it. I don't know what the right way is. I only know that I have total freedom to do it my way. Jeff and I do have different needs and views concerning Joshua's hours of sleep and this is reflected in our attitudes and behavior toward Joshua. Joshua knows our attitudes differ; but while he has occasionally worked to use this to his own advantage ("But Dad, *Mommy* lets me stay up late"), he is quickly reminded that different houses mean different rules.

Parents who are living together often have different rules and different expectations for their children. These differences seem clearer in co-parenting, and, more importantly, there is no bickering over who's in charge. You both are, at separate times. In the co-parenting situation, parents can discuss differences, be open-minded and learn from each other's ideas and methods, and then go on doing it their own way if they so choose, without any serious disruption in the co-parenting system.

One value that Jeff and I do share is in discussing our differences and learning from each other. The focus in these discussions is our parenting of Joshua. There is a freedom in our relationship to express these kinds of feelings to each other without much repercussion. Problem areas have arisen and have been smoothed out over the years; I want to alert you to some of them as you think about co-parenting.

Jeff and I have had our share of competitive and jealous feelings toward each other. Some of these feelings have to do with vacations. I felt resentful because Jeff was able to take Joshua away on several nice trips during the first years of our separation. My excuse for why I didn't do those things with Joshua was that I didn't have the money, whereas Jeff did. Some of that may be valid. But what was probably more relevant is the fact that Jeff is the kind of person who organizes things well in advance. He will write to reserve a campsite at a beautiful state park months ahead of time. He will get all the camping gear organized and get up the energy to take Joshua camping. Or he will hear about a family-oriented camp in the wilds of New Hampshire, will write for information, again make the reservations, and get there. It is hard for me to do those things.

During the first summer of our separation, Jeff and Joshua went camping for two weeks. I didn't hear from them all that time; by the end of the two weeks, I had developed a fine case of paranoia. There was no way I could get in touch with them, and since I hadn't gotten a phone call or a postcard during what seemed like an endless amount of time, I thought for sure that Jeff had decided to leave the country with Joshua and never return. Prior to that time I had thought I trusted Jeff implicitly. What I saw then was that I needed some attention from him at an especially sensitive time for me—when he was away with Joshua. When Jeff did return, much to my relief, I told him about my feelings and my need to have some form of communication from him during his times away with Joshua. There has been no problem with that since then. Out of our respect for each other and our continuing desire to make co-parenting work well, we are easily able to meet each other's needs to stay in touch with Joshua, especially when he is with the other parent.

Other jealous feelings have come up for me. Barbara, Jeff's girlfriend, has a child from a previous marriage. My view of what constitutes a family is that when Joshua is with Jeff and Barbara and her son Ricky, he is part of a family. When he is with me, I feel there is something missing. (This is *my* stereotype, remember.) Recently, Joshua and I went out to dinner with a male friend of mine whom Joshua is fond of. They were sitting close to each other in the restaurant, obviously enjoying each other's company. Someone made a remark to us indicating that they thought we were mother, father, and child. The three of us had a good laugh about it, and then I said that I bet that happens to Joshua all the time when he is with Jeff and Barbara. He said yes, it does, people think Barbara is his mother and Ricky is his little brother. "But we all know different," he said. We continued to talk about what things look like from the outside and how that might differ from what we know the truth to be. I had never been jealous of Joshua's relationship with Barbara (more on that in a bit), and this made it clear to me that Joshua was aware how people, including me, need to see things in order to make them regular or normal. Before this incident I had been too afraid of my own feelings to talk with Joshua about this; since that time we have discussed many other such delicate areas.

Jealousy comes up often. I expected to be jealous about Jeff's relationship with Barbara, but I certainly didn't count on all the other people I could be jealous of if I wanted to. What used to be difficult for me emotionally was facing up to the fact that Joshua has a relationship with Barbara's parents—that he has, in effect, another set of grandparents. One day he was busy making a birthday present for Barbara's father. This was something I thought he should do for *my* father, not hers. Joshua and I talked about how he knew a lot of people I didn't know; since then he has shared with me much more of his life that exists separate from me. Because I opened the topic for discussion, he saw that he could talk about more too. One day, after he had come back from visiting Barbara's parents' house, he told me he went swimming in Frank and Lizzy's pool. Then he started laughing because he realized that I didn't even know who Frank and Lizzy were. It was an easy experience for both of us.

People often ask me if I am jealous of my son's relationship with another woman. Or, they naturally assume that I am. Well, I haven't been so far. I always think of Barbara as a plus in Joshua's life, another loving person—and I know he can't have too much of that. Barbara is an artistic person who has contributed to Joshua's life in a way that I can't. She has made beautiful things for Joshua and has assisted him in being more creative himself. I know that I have my own special gifts and talents, but this just isn't one of them. People often wonder if Joshua gets confused about who his mother is. This is absurd. Joshua knows who his mother is and that person is me.

Not only is Jeff still part of my family, but Barbara is very much part of my world too. She and I don't see each other often, but when we do there is an ease and comfort between us. Of course she knows a lot about me through Jeff and through Joshua. It makes for easier co-parenting, too, to like the people whom your child spends so much of his time with. I have never met Barbara's parents, but feel warmly toward them, knowing that they really care about Joshua and include him in their family. I also am aware of the obvious pleasure Joshua gets out of his relationship with them.

Another aspect of this situation is that Joshua and Ricky are very close. Joshua has said that he considers Ricky a brother. Although I have met Ricky a few times, I feel as if I barely know him; this has begun to feel strange to me. Jeff recently asked me if I would take care of Ricky for a few days so he and Barbara could go away. At first I was dumbfounded and found it altogether laughable that he would even ask me. Then, as I began to consider the possibility, it seemed like a reasonable request. But I decided not to do it then and told Jeff and Barbara to ask me again sometime. They did ask me again, for one night this time, and I took care of Ricky quite easily. I found that there was room in my life for loving feelings toward Ricky, and I liked the feeling of being as big a person as I knew I could be. I also loved seeing the warmth and closeness that existed between Joshua and Ricky. I wouldn't choose to do that often, mainly because I don't choose to have that much direct involvement with Jeff and Barbara's relationship, and this is certainly not something that is a prerequisite for effective co-parenting. Yet it is a way of looking at things that is expansive and that says anything is possible to work out. However—and this is a big however—as much fun as I had being with Joshua and Ricky, that's as depressed as I was for the next few days. It's hard to push through our own barriers. I felt lonely, and was jealous again of the family unit of Jeff, Barbara, Joshua, and Ricky. So, along with the benefits to me of being with Ricky, there were definitely costs. And I'd still dō it again.

For some people who co-parent, it is very difficult to work out dealing with other relationships both in their own lives and in the lives of their ex-spouses. Jerilyn relates the following:

Co-parenting is much more complex now because it's becoming much more like two complete households. There's another person for the children to deal with at John's house and in my life there's another person also. The children have been reacting to that—it's been a strain, and I have been reacting to it. I've been reacting to the idea of another woman's being my children's mother.

Basically, that makes me feel threatened, the feeling of being displaced. It also makes me very watchful of what Susan is doing with them. I'm afraid that she's going to influence them or act towards them in ways that will influence them and that I don't like, or that I want to protect them from. She's a nice person, but she's very young and inexperienced. I have, I think, some real grounds for feeling that she can't handle the situation very well, that she doesn't know what she's doing. What John has told me is that Susan recognizes that I'm their mother and she doesn't really want to take that role; but I see her doing everything she can to be really involved with them. She puts out a lot of energy in that direction. The kids seem to feel like she's getting between them and John. For one thing, they complain that when they're with her and John, she takes the lead from John. They feel, "Where's daddy? What's happening?" I can imagine that he's in a very sticky position trying to get that one together.

Susan ignores me. She addresses her remarks to the children and to John, but she never looks me in the eye. She never talks to me and she acts like I don't exist. We all got together for a meeting and tried to talk about the situation, but it was not really satisfactory. I told Susan that if she was going to be with John, she had to have a relationship with me, and, whether she liked it or not, that's the situation. I made it clearly understood whose role was what and that I was the mother. Since then, I've felt at times that I want my children back and that I don't want her to be their mother even half the time. But I've also begun to feel more realistic and less uptight about it. And since our meeting, Susan and I haven't had any real interaction at all.

One problem in my situation now concerns birthdays, mine to be specific. Jeff was never good about celebrating my birthday during the ten years of our relationship, though somehow I fully expected that he would make sure I'd get a present from Joshua. For the first few years after our separation, things didn't work out according to my expectations. Either my birthday was totally forgotten, or Jeff and Joshua were away on vacation and I didn't get a card in the mail. One year I did get a present when they returned from vacation, but it wasn't the same for me. Because my birthday was not being celebrated in the style I envisioned, and Joshua was never with me for my birthday (since it's in the two-week period in August when he is away with Jeff), I talked with Jeff about rearranging our summer vacation schedules. Jeff suggested that instead of reorganizing plans, Joshua and I celebrate my birthday before its actual date so I wouldn't feel neglected and cheated out of Joshua's presence on an important day to me. This seemed like a good solution to me—so good in fact that Joshua and I began to celebrate my birthday in June and carried right on through until mid-August. In this, as in other situations, solutions exist to problems that seemed unsolvable. In order to find them, both parents need to retain an open mind and assume that it is possible to discover creative solutions for the problems that arise as a result of new and changing life styles.

In the preceding pages I have written about the relationships that are important to Jeff because these relationships, in a co-parenting situation, are important to me as well. It would surely be possible for me not to like Barbara, not to have anything at all to do with her son and her parents, and still co-parent effectively. These people do, however, encompass Joshua's world and I choose to include them in mine.

Where are you right now in relationship to your ex-spouse? Is this comfortable with you? If you have just separated you will feel quite differently toward your ex-spouse than you would if you have been divorced for several years. There are no rights and wrongs concerning feelings. I would encourage you, though, to nurture a relationship with a minimum of conflict. Life is just a whole lot easier when you can put aside the bad feelings you might have toward one another and concentrate on the ways you can improve your level of communication.

Ian and I bend over backward not to get into squabbles with each other about where Jessie spends her time. We know several couples who always squabble over the kids, about who's going to be able to spend more time with their children. Just about any issue you name, they don't agree on. Ian and I are very very careful not to get involved in that. If some point of conflict does come up, such as one night when each thought the other was going to have Jessie, or something like that, we'll both defer to the other: you first—no, you first. We don't want to get involved in petty squabbling because it's so destructive. [Carolyn]

Your relationship with your ex-spouse, then, can be what you want it to be. You can be close, share a lot, and communicate with ease. Or you can be distant and keep your relationship on a strictly business level. What feels comfortable for both of you is what is important. Your goal now is to maintain a relationship that not only allows you, but encourages and supports you, to be the best parents you can be to your child.

The Child's Adjustment

*I have co-parents, right Mom? Then I guess
I'm a co-son. No. I'm a co-child.*

Joshua Galper, age 7½

Separation and divorce is a difficult transition for children to experience. This is so regardless of the living arrangements parents create for them. All children experience some degree of anger, sadness, depression, or confusion at first. They are upset when their parents separate, and their lives may be in a state of upheaval. As everything around them is changing, the uncertainty of their world at this time can cause pain and distress.

Children show signs of their pain in different ways. Some children may develop sleeping problems, others may become withdrawn, others may have trouble concentrating on their school work. The extent of these difficulties varies with individual children, their ages, and specific home situations. A child who has experienced his parents' fighting may feel great relief after their separation, now that the fighting is over and there is peace at home. Yet he may also feel sad that his parents had to separate. A young child whose parents did not argue, on the other hand, may be confused about why his parents had to separate, and he may have trouble understanding why this disruption in his life was necessary.

Children have to explain to their friends where the now-absent parent went, and why. They need to figure out for themselves what the changes in their living situations will mean. Most important, they need time to adjust to the newness of it all.

It is difficult to distinguish the effects of a co-parenting situation on a child from the effects of other custody arrangements after separation and divorce. There is no evidence to suggest that co-parenting presents more problems for the child; there is no hard research to document the outcome for a child of co-parenting. What I can say, then, is that adjustment is always a matter of degree, whether the parents are separated and one parent has visitation rights, whether they are co-parenting, or whatever the arrangement.

We tend to forget that children also go through behavior which is age-appropriate, and that they may be doing this at the time a separation is taking place. For instance, nightmares are a common occurrence for a four- or five-year-old child. But for a child who is four and whose parents have recently separated, nightmares are seen as abnormal and as a sign that the child is having great difficulty adjusting to the separation. That may be true. What is also true is that all children have nightmares at a certain time in their development.

One reaction that people expect from a child adjusting to co-parenting is confusion. Joshua was four years old when Jeff and I separated. Our first arrangement (as I describe in Chapter II) meant that Joshua changed houses every other night. He was indeed confused by the whole situation. His behavior patterns changed drastically; he became unhappy, angry, and depressed. To be sure, he had a difficult time in the first few months after our separation. Yet my assumption is that he would have been in pain about it no matter what our living arrangement was. Now, and for a couple of years now, he is not pained or confused, and knows exactly where he lives at all times.

On the other hand, my friend Carolyn reports that her daughter has never seemed confused in reaction to her living arrangements. "Jessie wants to know who's going to pick her up on a given night; and as long as she's told, she doesn't seem anxious about where she's going to be."

Not at all confusing to Joshua was the fact that Jeff and I both continued to love him very much. Co-parenting allowed for greater continuity and intimacy in Joshua's relationship with each of us. He knew he was valued and cared about by both of us and that he was not responsible for the separation. He did not experience feelings of being abandoned or rejected by one of us. He did not have to experience the loss of one parent. On the contrary, he experienced us separately as being willing to spend more time with him in a more intense way than we had done in the past.

In the first few months after our separation, Joshua would be very upset if our schedule changed in some way, even if it only changed slightly. Jeff usually brought him to my house at 10 A.M. on Sundays. Occasionally, Jeff would want to bring Joshua over a bit later, and Jeff reported that the extra hour they would spend together would be a very tense and anxious time for Joshua. Aware of the time at a young age, he was keyed up for coming to my house and did not like the routine changed. It was important to him to have predictability in his life, to know that at 10 A.M. on Sundays he *would* be at my house. Over the years Joshua has become more flexible; any extra time spent at one house or the other is not a problem any more. It has taken time for Joshua to see that there can be some leeway within his routine, and to feel comfortable with that.

The children were eight and eleven when we separated. Our first schedule was that they would spend one week with me and then one week with their father. We were not rigid about sticking to that

70

schedule and both kids told us that it was especially hard when we changed things around. Then they both requested that they spend longer periods of time at each house, so that now they spend two weeks with me and two weeks with their father. It sounds easy now, but the process was a very hard one for all of us. [Lois]

Children need stability, and stability comes in a variety of forms. I do not assume that stability equals one primary parent and one primary home. Stability can also mean a relationship of constancy and permanence with two parents in two separate homes. A child's life may be temporarily disrupted by separation, but it can become stabilized again in new forms. Children need to know that their needs will be taken care of. They need to be able to predict that their lives will go on in much the same way as before their parents' separation. Children need to identify positively with both parents—not be pushed into situations in which they are forced to express loyalty to one parent over another.

An issue for all children is learning to live with differences. Children living in intact families are very aware of their parents' differing views on child raising, since much of this is cause for argument in many homes. They will use this difference as ammunition in the conflict between parents. "But Mommy said I *can* stay up late tonight." "But Daddy said I *can* get a new toy tomorrow."

After a separation takes place, differences seem clearer to the child. He learns very quickly what the expectations are for his behavior when he is with one parent or the other. Some rules belong in mother's house but not in father's. Father is strict about some things that mother doesn't care about. When a child is with his father, he understands that he can behave in ways which might be unacceptable to his mother. As the differences become more obvious, there is no bickering about them, so the child can more easily accept the fact that in two homes there may be two different sets of rules.

Similarly, parents do not have to have the same life style in order to co-parent effectively, nor do they have to agree on how to deal with their children under each set of circumstances. We have all learned how to modify our behavior to suit a situation, and children learn this too.

Kathy, age 13, says that she knows her parents do things differently:

I just take what my father has to say, and take what my mom has to say too. I know what's good and what's not, so I just take what they both have to say and I figure things out for myself.

Joshua has learned to accept certain differences between Jeff and me. About two years after we had separated, Joshua asked me to put a treat in his lunch box every day. I said I didn't want to do that, that I would give him some fruit but not candy. He then said that when Dad makes his lunch, he gets a health-store-type candy bar, and I wouldn't do that. When I make his lunch, I am willing to make him peanut butter and jelly sandwiches every day, which he likes, but Dad is not willing to do that. So, he said, in each situation he gets something that he does want and something that he doesn't want.

This was a small thing, yet it told me much about Joshua's acceptance of the fact that Jeff and I do things differently and that he can get something good for himself within those differences.

All children sometimes work at playing one parent off against the other. Children living in nuclear families do it, and children whose parents are separated or divorced do it. Children of co-parents have an extra whammy to their play: saying that they want to live permanently with the other parent. One time when Joshua was angry at me, he announced that he wanted to live with Jeff all the time. I don't remember what my reaction was, except that I didn't panic. I probably said something fairly non-committal and let the moment pass. What happens more often if Joshua is upset with either Jeff or me is that he will want to telephone the other parent, ostensibly to complain about the maltreatment he's received.

Recently, Joshua called me early one Sunday morning to complain about the breakfast Jeff had prepared—blueberry pancakes. Joshua likes his pancakes plain. There was nothing else in the house for him to eat. No cold cereal, no egg, no toast. He sounded truly pitiful. While I wasn't sure about everything that was going on, I did know that I would listen to him, encourage him to work it out with Jeff, but not side with him about what a terrible father he had. In discussing this later with Jeff, it seemed clear that Joshua was using his call to me as a way to threaten Jeff, or to push him to act in a different way. Jeff told him he could call me, that he could call me whenever he wanted to, but that he didn't like the idea of Joshua calling me about this because he was behaving in an obnoxious way. Jeff also had faith that I know not to undermine him in relation to Joshua. In fact, we each have faith that the other parent is generally on target in relating to Joshua. We both know what to say to be open to Joshua, to be available to listen to him, and yet not support his complaints about the other parent. The situation for us is usually quite obvious and stands out quite clearly for us to evaluate. Joshua went without breakfast that Sunday morning.

Ambivalence is an affliction of children as well as adults. On one occasion, Joshua announced that he wanted to live with me full time and spend time with Jeff only occasionally. He wanted to follow a system that Barbara and Ricky used, where Ricky would be with his Dad every other weekend, and one week night every other week. He was angry at Jeff for being too strict around bedtime—which he saw as Barbara's influence on Jeff. I think Joshua was also reacting to a difficult time that he and Barbara were having in their own relationship; it was painful for him to be with her. Joshua was jealous of the amount of time Jeff spent with Barbara and was feeling like he was getting the short end of the stick. I encouraged him to talk to Jeff about it, which he did. At the same time, Joshua and Barbara talked about some of their feelings toward each other, and the situation eased considerably.

I think my relationship with Josh has had its ups and downs. And I remember investing a lot of energy in Josh when I first met him, and I felt like I was really involved with him. But then there have been times when it's been hard for me and Josh. He really has a sense of his right to Jeff, in relationship to me—for example, how much time he's entitled to. Sometimes this interferes with my plans, and I've been aware of getting into power struggles with Josh. We don't get into fights—I don't fight with him—but there is a tension sometimes. Yet this is irregular on both our parts, and it's not the way we are together most of the times. I love Joshie and I feel he's a part of my life.[Barbara]

Around the time Joshua said he wanted to live with me full time, his school was offering tickets to a concert series on Saturday mornings. As Joshua is very excited about music, I thought it would be something he would enjoy. He agreed that he'd like it. But then he came back and said, "No way I'm going to those concerts. Saturday is the only full day I have with Daddy, because Friday is school and Sunday morning I come to you, so I'm not going to those concerts." He was able to fully accept the reality of his world and make meaningful choices for himself.

In the beginning of our separation, I rarely called at all for the entire two weeks the kids were at their father's. I think now I stayed away too much. My ex-husband, on the other hand, used to call the kids every day when they were at my place, and I had to ask him to cut down on that. My daughter requested this too. She doesn't want me calling her when she's at her father's. She wants to be totally with the parent whom she's with for those two weeks. My son does call me occasionally, just to chat. [Lois]

A fact of co-parenting is that the children have two distinct places of residence. This is the reality that most clearly differentiates co-parenting from the more traditional custody arrangements. Both homes are primary: I don't assume that my home is Joshua's real home, or that when he goes to Jeff's he is only visiting.

A child in this situation needs to deal with what it means to him to have two homes. It certainly is different from the way most of his friends live. All children whose parents are living apart need to respond to their friends' questions about the absent parent. Joshua has had to tell his friends to call him at his father's house on certain days. He has had to explain to the neighborhood children why he gets on the school bus at a different stop on Friday mornings (he comes from his father's house then). I overheard a conversation he had with a friend who wanted to know where Jeff was and why he wasn't living with me any more. Joshua answered that his parents weren't happy living together, that Jeff lived nearby, and "I'm tired of this discussion—let's play." Joshua has been able to present his living arrangements to his friends in a straightforward, clear-cut way, and they have understood where to find him on which days.

"It's hard for me to explain to my friends," said ten-year-old Sean:

I tell them that my mother and father live in different houses and that I go to their house every half a week. And they say, oh yeah? Most of the people that I'm telling, their parents live together. So it's hard to explain, 'cause they're not used to it. To me, though, it's not co-parenting or anything like that. It's just family.

Two separate residences mean two sets of toys, clothes, playmates, and living facilities, environmental differences, and a different adult to relate to in each home. Occasionally when Joshua is in my house he wants a toy that is residing at Jeff's. This kind of thing is not an insurmountable problem, yet children do have to deal with it. For some, toys mean more than mere playthings. I am coming to see the issue of Joshua's caring about where his toys are as symbolic of his feelings toward his living arrangement. Joshua used to complain frequently about wanting something that was at Jeff's house, and he'd get pretty upset about it too. In recent months, however, he has made no request to get something he left at Jeff's. Joshua is now much more in charge of getting together all the things he needs to bring from one house to another. If he does forget to bring something he wants, he knows that within a few days he'll be back with the toy he wanted, and this seems to be fine with him now.

Co-Parenting

Rachael got a dollhouse for Chanukah from her grandmother. We asked her where she was going to keep it, at my apartment or at her father's house. She said she'd keep it at her grandmother's, because she didn't have as much to play with there. But I sensed something was not right—and that was that she couldn't figure out who would be offended by whatever she might decide. If she decided on my place, maybe her Daddy would be hurt. Or if she said his place, would I be upset? It ended up that she decided to bring it to my apartment, and that was fine with her Dad too. [Marilynn]

Co-parenting allows a child to get his needs met in a variety of situations. Children who live in two homes get to experience many different people and different ways of living, and have a great opportunity to have a broad, expansive childhood. As my friend Gloria put it:

My kids are happy and healthy. They have almost more adults to relate to than I have. Many of their parents' friends are their own friends. This gives them the opportunity to have a lot of alternative role models, which I think is fabulous. They know men who are macho and men who enjoy cooking and caretaking. They know wives, mothers, single adults, students, professionals, workers, folks on welfare, heart surgeons, and freelance artists. There is an enormously extended family of people whom they love and who love them. I couldn't think of a more fun way to grow up.

Is it asking a lot to want children to accept living in two different places? I used to think so. Now I see it as part of a package. Living at two residences allows a child whose parents have separated to relate to each of his parents continually and to know each of them intimately. He can use the fact that he has toys in two homes to his advantage. He gets to play with things he hasn't seen for a while, and to feel almost as if they are new toys all over again.

Joshua has had fun using the co-parenting situation to his advantage. It's as if he knows that there are some distinct benefits to living in two homes. When one such benefit is apparent, he will make the most of it. Jeff and I oblige him in this regard; we are, for example, both pleased to be tooth fairies. We know, too, that co-parenting presents Joshua with some challenging situations; so when there is a situation (like losing a tooth) that lends itself to an extra for Joshua, we are both glad to be a part of it. And it is out of love, not guilt, that we encourage Joshua to take advantage of co-parenting when he can.

Transition times are difficult for all children who spend time with one parent and then another. Mothers in traditional custody situations often report that when their children return from a weekend or a day with Daddy, they are very difficult to live with. It takes a while to readjust to routine. Similarly, in co-parenting, parents report difficulties at the time of switching from house to another.

Early in our separation, when Joshua would come to my house on Sunday mornings after he had been with Jeff for three-and-a-half days, there was usually some period of adjustment he would go through with me. His mood was not happy, he needed instant attention from me, and he was difficult and testy very often. His irritable behavior would calm down after a few hours, but transition times were always tense for Joshua and me until the two of us eased into being with each other again. Such was not the case when Joshua went to Jeff's house on Thursday afternoons. He seemed to ease into being at Jeff's house more readily, probably because he was already in the midst of a regular pattern, coming from a school afternoon and heading toward a school night before waking up the next morning to catch the bus. There was some external structure to the time when he shifted homes from mine to Jeff's, but very little such structure when he came to my house on a Sunday morning. In recent months, however, I have noticed a great decline in the amount of upset behavior Joshua experiences when he returns to my house. He moves into the neighborhood more easily, seems calmer, and is better able to relate to me in happy, comfortable ways. Is it possible that it has taken Joshua almost three years to adjust to his situation? Maybe so. I think that he was adjusting all along, but perhpas not in ways that I always

Co-Parenting

found acceptable. We need to give our children the freedom to progress at their own pace and in their own style.

As adults we have gone through various stages of behavior and feelings in relation to our separation and divorce, and there is no reason to think that this is not the same for our children. We have been depressed, angry, bitter, unhappy. And then we have come to make our peace with our lives. For some of us this has taken a shorter period of time than for others. But one way is no more or less valid than another. Joshua's depression lasted for about six months after our separation. Mine lasted for over a year. I do not imagine that, if given a choice, Joshua would choose his present life style. He probably wishes that Jeff and I would get back together. But within the context of our separation and divorce, he has learned to accept his way of life.

My friend Mike, his mommy and daddy are divorced, and I don't think he minds, he doesn't act like it. And I sometimes think in my head, how nice it would be if Mommy and Daddy got back together again. [Rachael, age 6½]

I have clothes at both my father's and my mother's house, and I go to my mother's house on Wednesday, and go to my father's house from my mother's house on Saturday. My father got married again, so I have two step brothers, Matthew and Steve, at my father's house. I have one dog there, and some fish. We have a cat here. Mostly it's been all right for me but I sort of wish that we were all living together again. [Ari, age 8]

I don't expect that Joshua's life from here on will be smooth sailing. I think that at different times of his life some of his old feelings will return, as is true for all of us. When we are feeling depressed and things aren't going well for us at a particular point in time, we can think about how different our lives would have been *if only*. If only we hadn't divorced. If only we hadn't married in the first place. So much anger and turmoil get stirred up by all those old feelings.

As children go through different developmental stages, their old feelings of uncertainty about their lives may return. This is a natural part of accepting and adjusting to their way of life. They get angry at you all over again for having separated in the first place. They may go through a period of depression and withdrawal similar to ones they might have experienced at the time of your separation. It takes time for children to deal with all the feelings brought on by their parents' separation and divorce, as well as the feelings which come up concerning how their parents have chosen to continue parenting.

One of the effects on children living in a co-parenting situation is that they become extremely close to both parents. Relationships become more strongly bonded as a result of a more intimate interaction between parent and child. There is no one to interfere for you, no one to take over for you in a tense situation. My relationship with Joshua now has a depth to it that did not exist when we all lived togather. Other parents I've talked to have reported the same kind of thing, and some even worry about the closeness they feel with their children.

At times I've made mistakes, putting too much weight on my relationship with my daughter. She really is the most important person in my life and I worry sometimes about feeling too close to her. I don't know how other parents feel about their kids, but I do know that she is just about everything there is in the world to me. And I think that's unhealthy for a mother to love a child so much. I worry if I'm depending on her too much and treating her too much like my friend and not enough like my little girl.[Deborah]

Many children whose parents separate complain a lot about aches and pains. From my talks with other separated parents, this seems to be a fairly common response to the disruptions going on in the children's lives. Soon after Jeff and I separated, Joshua began to tell me that his brain hurt, or that he felt weak. This subsided after a while, and another kind of behavior developed. It seemed that whenever Jeff would go away on a trip and our schedule was changed somewhat, Joshua would get sick. Not just a cold, but a high fever (104 or 105 degrees was his usual), occasionally a strep throat. It took a while for me to make the connection between Jeff's absence and Joshua's illnesses. Once in a while it would happen when I traveled, but not usually. When I think about Joshua's illnesses now, it may be that Joshua was reacting to Jeff's absence by insuring that he could stay close to me. I began to talk to Joshua about what I thought was happening, saying that I noticed he got sick whenever Dad went away. He agreed that he did. I didn't go into my interpretations about why this was so. I have noticed, though, that Joshua's illnesses have decreased considerably and that he is more comfortable and secure now in our living situation. He is able to be more flexible around schedules, vacations, and one parent's absence from the routine for a short period of time. He doesn't need to get sick when Jeff goes away now because he has had enough experience to see that Jeff always comes back.

What are the behavorial characteristics of children who live in co-parenting arrangements? Generally, many divorced parents with traditional custody arrangements report that their children show a greater sense of independence. As single parents, they need help from their children in order to accomplish the daily living tasks; they therefore encourage their children to be more self-reliant. Co-parents indicate the same kind of behavior in their children.

I recently had a conversation with Paula, a close friend, who spoke about some characteristics of Joshua's that she thought were unusual. "He's much more worldly wise than most kids his age. He can negotiate his way in strange places, handle money well, and talks to adults in a mature way." Paula also said that she didn't know if these characteristics were a result of co-parenting or a result of who Joshua is and would be no matter what his life style. She described Joshua as much more mature and independent than most children his age, and then also worried that he was having to grow up too fast. "Where's his childhood?"

One evening when Paula was at my house, Joshua was talking about a new tooth that felt loose. I asked him when his next dentist appointment was, since he goes to the dentist with Jeff. He answered immediately, saying it was October 14th. Paula was dumbfounded. (Her daughter, who is Joshua's age, would not have the least notion of when her next appointment might be.)

Of course I know what my schedule is. I have to know. I have to figure out what things I'll need for the next few nights if it's a day I go to my other house. Besides, it's fun for me to plan all that stuff.[Gregory, age 9.]

After having adjusted to your separation, your children may or may not find it difficult to spend time on certain occasions with both parents together. Indeed, some differences of opinion do exist concerning the soundness of spending time together. You and your ex-spouse may be feeling good about each other and may want to talk for a while when your children make the switch from one house to another. Should you have a cup of coffee together, with the children around? What will they think? Will they hope you're making plans to get back together? Will they leave you alone to talk, or hang around and make it difficult for you to have a calm conversation? Some people say that children should get used to the fact that their parents are no longer married and that any time they spend together is time feeding a child's fantasies, hoping his parents will get back together. This seems like a rather hard-nosed approach to me. Jeff and Joshua and I have spent some time together which has been especially pleasant, and some time together which has been especially difficult. We have all learned, however, what kind of activity makes for a good time. So we have learned to plan such times accordingly.

Soon after we separated, whenever Jeff would stay at my house for a while when he was bringing Joshua over, there would be no peace. Joshua would be demanding of our attention, would be intrusive, and would be totally difficult to be with. In a talk with me Joshua said that he didn't like it when

Dad stayed at my house but that it was okay for the three of us to eat out in a restaurant together, or else be at Dad's house together. He didn't go on to explain why, though it seemed obvious that Jeff's presence in my house reminded him of the time when Jeff used to live here, and that was, apparently, painful for Joshua to witness.

The few times that we got together in other places during the first year after our separation were not particularly pleasant either. Since that time, however, with Joshua's participation in the discussion of whether or not we will get together, and where, these times have been really nice for all of us. Occasionally we will have dinner together, usually a spur of the moment decision. Jeff and I plan and attend Joshua's birthday parties together, and then we have another celebration for just the three of us.

The three of us did go out to dinner once, and Jessie loved it. And it was a chance for Ian and me to get caught up on stuff. And in fact we were talking about adult stuff, not Jessie-related stuff. And she said, "Listen, you people are here to take me out to dinner, so you talk to me!" But when I pushed for us to do that again, and it was easy for us all to have lunch together at her day-care center, Ian said no. And the reason that he gave was that he thought that would get Jessie's expectations up about us getting back together again. I don't think that was the real reason. I think that it's still hard for him to be with me and maybe it's painful in the sense of reminding him too much of the family that we had.

For Jessie's birthday this year Ian came to my house and my parents and sisters were there. Jessie loved it. She felt that her people had come together for her and she was really clear that at the end of the day Ian was going to go home to his house. I think when she says, "I'd like you to get back together," she knows that's not going to happen, she's just expressing that feeling.[Carolyn]

Joshua's school has an annual Spring Thing, which for the past few years we have all attended together. As it is a time of families' being together, it seems reasonable for Joshua to want both of his parents to be with him. And both Jeff and I want to be part of that experience. Any discomfort that Joshua used to have with the three of us being together doesn't occur any more. When it is time for us to leave the threesome unit, he goes off with the parent he came with, does not ask for the time to be extended, and he behaves in an entirely appropriate way throughout our time together. I feel good about Jeff, Joshua, and me being able to spend some low-key times together. No one pretends that we are like any other family out for a family outing. We know exactly who we are — two parents who love their child very much and one child who loves being with his parents.

Four years have passed since Jeff and I first separated and I am pleased with the way Joshua feels about his life. It becomes clearer to me all the time now that co-parenting works for Joshua. A few weeks ago Jeff brought Joshua to my house and stayed for a few minutes to chat. As Jeff got ready to leave, Joshua said, "Goodbye Daddy, Hello Mommy," in a cheery tone of voice. It was as if he was announcing the transfer from Jeff to me and it was a satisfying moment for all of us. We knew his meaning, in the literal sense as a family, and in the psychological sense of what we each had gone through in order to feel good about our lives now. We were pleased with ourselves, Jeff and Joshua and I, and proud of our familial abilities to continue to be caring about one another four years after the formal separation took place.

We as parents—all separated parents—need to trust ourselves, each other, and our children. We need to look at our children and allow ourselves to hear what they are saying and understand what their behavior is telling us. We also need to think clearly about what behavior is age appropriate and what might be related to a separation and divorce in the family. And we need to give our children the time and opportunity to express their feelings in whatever way is comfortable for them, and to accept those feelings.

The child's adjustment to separation and divorce in general, and to co-parenting in particular, does not occur overnight. But with greater speed and flexibility than you might imagine, most children are able to take control over their new ways of life. They learn their schedules easily, are clear about the times they go to each home, and are able to explain the way they live to their friends. While they may, like most children whose parents have separated or divorced, wish their parents would live together again, they understand that this will not happen. They also understand that with co-parenting they have a special arrangement. They have the opportunity to continue their loving relationship with both parents. They do not feel neglected or abandoned. They feel truly loved.

What the Professionals Say

I think the biggest variable is how clear the parents are with the child about the reality of life and about the reality of the arrangements. I don't think that having two houses in and of itself is disruptive, in the same way that I don't think having one house in and of itself is stabilizing.

Roslyn Weinberger, M.S.W.,
Clinical Social Worker

Co-parenting is a word that is not in the dictionary. As few as five years ago, it was not a word that had much meaning to many people. Even terms such as joint custody or shared custody were not part of the common terminology which people used when talking about living arrangements for children after separation or divorce.

As a result of the large increase in the number of marriages that have ended in separation or divorce, professionals have begun to look at the effects of single-parent custody on both children and the parents. Some minimal research has been done for traditional custody arrangements, but very little in the area of co-parenting. What the studies do point to is that children need a relationship with both parents. When children do not see their fathers for long periods of time, they are unhappy, despondent, and often do not perform well in school. Children need to know that they have not been abandoned or rejected by the parent who leaves the home. Fathers—usually the parent who leaves the home—feel cut off from their children and greatly fear being shut out of their children's lives. Fathers who are involved with their children feel good about themselves, although their experience is that it is a struggle to maintain close contact.

The research that has been done reveals that the more the parents can relate to each other decently, the better the adjustment of the child will be to the change in their marriage. Further, this work suggests that even though children may not be happy about the new situation, they enjoy having intimate contact with both parents after separation or divorce. One psychologist I know who has spoken with many children in a co-parenting situation sees evidence of their relatively easy adjustment to living in two separate environments. An additional aspect of research to date is that single parents who have 24-hour-a-day responsibility for their children find it to be an overwhelming, burdensome task which does not promote good relationships between them.

While it is reasonable to suggest that co-parenting can be a positive alternative to the more traditional forms of custody arrangements, there is a great deal of resistance to the idea of co-parenting on the part of many professionals in the fields of mental health and law. This resistance is not based on sound, hard facts, but rather on theories about what is presumably in the best interests of the child. Such theories relate to social thought at any given time. Now, the commonly held view is that children need one home, and that that home should be with the mother.

Shades of opinion exist on this subject. A few practitioners such as social workers and psychologists do see some benefits to co-parenting. They have studied the results of arrangements in which the mother has custody and the father has visitation rights and have often found this situation to be problematic.

These professionals are open to considering co-parenting as an alternative. By and large, however, they are in the minority.

The major objections that many professionals have to co-parenting are the following:

—Children need one home and one primary parent.
—Children need roots. Co-parenting inhibits children from developing a sense of stability.
—Co-parenting is very confusing for children. They cannot cope with switching back and forth between two homes.
—Children who grow up in a co-parenting situation will have problems experiencing intimacy later in their lives.
—Co-parenting is a manipulation on the part of the parents to stay in touch with each other so that they can continue to act out their destructive relationship. Co-parenting doesn't allow parents to really separate from each other.

"A child needs one home," goes the common cry. Mental health professionals writing about post-divorce family life feel strongly that children need one primary parent in one home. Any other arrangement is destructive to a child's sense of himself and to his emotional well-being. After separation and divorce, many professionals contend, children need to establish continuity of relationship with one parent. This cannot happen successfully if they routinely move from one home to another, and from an emotional connection with one parent to an emotional connection with the other parent. *Beyond the Best Interests of the Child*, by Joseph Goldstein, Anna Freud, and Albert Solnit, is a book which popularized the notion that children are better off having minimal contact with the noncustodial parent. The authors feel that children should not have to deal at all with the ambiguities of a relationship with a noncustodial parent: "Children have difficulty in relating positively to, profiting from, and maintaining the contact with two psychological parents who are not in positive contact with each other. Loyalty conflicts are common and normal under such conditions and may have devastating consequences by destroying the child's positive relationships to both parents."

I think that the best thing for a child whose parents are divorced is to feel valued, loved, and cared for by both parents.

Having two homes allows for *more* continuity in the child's relationships with his parents. Co-parenting says to the child that whichever parent has moved out of the home will not move out of the child's life, and co-parenting assures the child that he is not responsible for the breakup of the marriage, as so many children imagine.

Yes, children's lives are disrupted by their parents' separation and divorce. But I think the disruption is greater if they have to stop relating to one parent completely—usually the father. Children have to face up to all kinds of questions then: "Where did my father go?" "Why don't I see him like I used to?" "Doesn't he love me?" "I miss my Daddy." Co-parenting provides a structure for both the child and parent in which to maintain a continual relationship, with perhaps even greater closeness than existed previously.

I have a sense that my need to be a primary parent is a kind of need inherent in men generally, but somehow it gets suppressed or otherwise thwarted in the lives of most men. [Jim]

In my experience and in the experience of the many parents I interviewed, children living in a co-parenting situation do not have difficulty relating to both parents. The children themselves talk about how much they value their relationships with both parents and they understand that they have something special in those relationships. Children report that they see more of their parents, especially their fathers, than they used to before the separation took place; and they are also very much aware of the fact that they spend more time with their fathers than do their friends who live in intact families.

Rebecca told me, "Being with you half the time and Dad half the time makes me feel more grateful for both of you." [Lois]

Dr. Naomi Reiskind, a child psychologist, suggests that in order for children to feel secure living in two homes they need to have a clear sense of what is expected of them in each home. They need to be told that there may be different rules and different behavior which would be acceptable in each home. As I discussed in the preceding chapter, children quickly learn what is appropriate in their distinct living environments and are able to adapt to that without any problem. The important consideration is talking openly about these differences with them. "Different houses, different rules."

Another issue raised by the skeptical professionals is that co-parenting inhibits children from developing a sense of stability. If they are constantly shifting from one home to another, they have no sense of belonging anywhere. They never establish roots, and never experience any security or trust in their environment. Children, they contend, cannot learn to be autonomous and capable unless they have a solid home base. That means one solid home, not two. Edith Atkin and Estelle Rubin, co-authors of *Part-Time Father*, state that, "Children need a base that is home. . . . This insistence that the children should believe they have two homes only emphasizes that they live in a divided world. [Father's] home can be a place where they feel comfortable, accepted, loved—in short, where they feel at home. But their home is at their mother's." The authors are describing a situation in which the mother has custody of the children and the father has visitation rights; they feel strongly that any form of shared custody is a bad idea.

My response to this criticism of co-parenting is that stability is created for children in many ways. Most importantly, stability will exist for children in their sense of anticipated continuity of being with each parent. Co-parenting enhances this sense. There are no wrenchings, no major breaks in the child's emotional ties with his parents. Parents are the stable force in any child's life, and co-parents remain very much an integral part of a child's life after separation or divorce by creating a stable environment in two separate households.

Continuity is created for the child when his parents live

relatively near each other so that he can go to the same school from either home. He can maintain his friendships no matter which home he is living in. For children between the ages of seven and twelve, Dr. Reiskind believes it is especially important to be able to maintain peer relationships. For instance, it might be quite disruptive socially for a child living in his mother's home for six months and then in his father's home for six months, assuming these homes are some distance apart geographically.

Clinical social worker Roslyn Weinberger, M.S.W., talked with me about children's need for a sense of security and predictability about their life:

If a child knows the schedule himself, knows the rhythms and can count on the adults to be there and can count on the adults not to catch him in the crossfire, then what does it matter how many homes he has?

Indeed, children *can* have stability and predictability in a co-parenting system. They can know which home they live in at which times, and they can rely on their parents to be there for them. All of the young children I spoke with knew their schedules precisely and seemed to be in strong command of their living situations.

Children establish roots very well in two homes. Before a separation they already have roots in their relationship with both parents, and these roots can flourish and take hold firmly through the co-parenting arrangement.

A third objection to co-parenting is that it is just very confusing for children. Many professionals claim that children must have consistency. A child should be able to say, "This is my bedroom. These are my books. When I do my homework tonight this is where I'll sit." The bedroom must be the same bedroom every night and the books must be in the same place every night. Any other arrangement increases the trauma of divorce for children. Uniform structure and a unilateral kind of security ease the pain of separation and divorce, it is contended, so children who grow up living in two homes will experience a great deal of confusion. This confusion can only lead to emotional disturbance later on in a child's life.

To be sure, some parents I've spoken with report that their children experienced some degree of confusion in the first few months of establishing a co-parenting system. They also report that this confusion abates fairly quickly. Other parents report that their children have never seemed confused by their living arrangements. (Joshua, remember, was somewhat confused initially.) If confusion does exist, it is minimized when there is a definite structure and regular schedule to the co-parenting arrangement. Children quickly learn what their schedules are and impress their parents and others around them with their ability to know just where they belong on what days.

It has always amazed me that my daughter, since the age of four when we separated, has always known what her schedule is. Sure we told her, and it's never basically changed, but she's nine now and she's never had to ask me, "What day is today? Where am I going tonight?" She's been in control of that from day one. [Stephanie]

Dr. Sidney Portnoy, Director of Children of Divorce (a counseling service for children and their families), believes that confusion in relation to living in two homes does not have to exist. A child can say to himself, "I am still me. These are still my parents. I have a desk and a bed and books in two homes." The clearer the parents are about the living arrangements, and the more direct they are about the workability of the co-parenting system, the less confusion the child will experience.

I believe one basic reason why people (professionals) assume that children will be confused by living in two homes is simply that co-parenting is still a new idea—most people are just not accustomed to dealing with it yet. Something new that is a radical departure from what is commonplace tends to elicit some confusion—confusion which, in this case, has apparently been misunderstood. For in my experience it is the adults who hear about co-parenting who get confused by it, not the children who live it.

Another major concern about children whose parents divorce is their capacity for intimacy. This relates not just to a co-parenting situation, but to all situations in which parents have formed new relationships. Suppose A and B have a child and then divorce; A and C marry; B and D marry. How many adults does the child now relate to as parent-figures? (What if A and C, or B and D, also divorce?) How many sets of grandparents does the child have? What do these changes imply about the child's ability to form intimate relationships? If there are so many adults in his life, does he relate in perhaps a less intimate way than if he had only two parents? Well, yes—according to the prevalent professional view. But there is no empirical evidence to document this point.

One should not equate the number of people in a child's life with his capacity for intimacy. My intuitive feeling (reinforced in my world of experience) is that having more people close to him does not diminish a child's capacity for intimacy. If a child does not have intimate relationships early in his life, that might diminish his capacity for intimacy. If a child relates to two parents only, I do not assume that he will be free of problems with intimacy. At some time we all have problems with intimacy, and we were all raised in a variety of settings and with a variety of relationships. If A and B, A and C, and B and D all relate to a child with closeness, warmth, and love—as A and B continue to parent—I think that child will have a rich and positive life experience. He will learn that he can be close to several adults and get his needs met by people other than his mother and father.

My kids are going to have a sense of family without a sense of it having to be an intact family. They're going to have a wider sense of who cares for them, and it isn't just Bill and me. It's Bill's wife, it's the people I live with—and these people take responsibility for the kids because they want to. I hope the kids are going to have a sense of a wider community of caring than some kids get from the narrow isolation of the nuclear family. [Judith]

The last point made by professionals who are opposed to co-parenting is that the system forces children to become go-betweens in their parents' never-ending battles. The co-parenting relationship is seen as an inability to let go and assert one's own adulthood, preventing the parents from becoming free to establish individual lives for themselves. From this viewpoint, co-parenting perpetuates a destructive relationship between ex-spouses, a relationship which provides two adults with an ongoing structure in which to continue their battles. In *Part-Time Father*, Atkin and Rubin maintain that the co-parenting arrangement "clearly . . . has more to do with the parents' need to keep their own fighting relationship going than with the child's best interests."

I totally agree that it would be a miserable situation for a child to be his parents' intermediary. There is a tendency, especially in the beginning of a separation, to pump a child for information about the ex-spouse. This should definitely be avoided. Parents need to deal with each other directly, asking each other what they want to know. Ms. Weinberger says, "The issue of getting caught in the crossfire is not made any greater by having a co-parenting arrangement than it is in the usual visitation arrangement. If parents are going to act out on the child and put the child in the middle, what the particular structure of the parenting is doesn't seem to matter."

Dr. Melvin Roman, Professor of Psychiatry at Albert Einstein College of Medicine in New York, has interviewed parents who share responsibility for raising their children. "When couples want to share custody of their children," Dr. Roman observes, "they are able to isolate out their mental conflicts from their parental responsibilities. In fact, it is not uncommon for joint custody parents to frankly admit their antipathy toward one another but to maintain, at the same time, that they do not intend to harm their children just because they might like to harm one another."

I think that a healthier resolution of a relationship which has ended in divorce exists in being able to say, yes, there are some things in this relationship that are troubling to me and that stir me up, but there are also some good things about this relationship, and I want to maintain that part. For some people who choose to co-parent, they might still be acting out of unhealthy motives—to stay close to each other in a way that does not produce growth and change for both parents. This need not be the case. People can learn to live with their ambivalent feelings in a relationship and they can use those feelings to learn about themselves and how they behave in a relationship. It would be easy to totally cut yourself off from the person you used to be married to. It would not be so easy if there are children involved, but certainly it would be easier not to co-parent. I think the healthier adaptation is for people to learn to tolerate ambivalence or conflicting feelings simultaneously. If you cut yourself off from your ex-spouse, that might mean you can't tolerate those parts of yourself that get stirred up by your ex-spouse. On the other hand, you will not be able to continue to experience what was good in your relationship.

We have a lot of structure and rules in our society. Either you are in a marriage or you're not, you have a home or you don't, you have a family or you don't. There is a human need for rules, but we have understood that in a limited way in the past. A co-parenting relationship allows ex-spouses to maintain the parent system which was part of their marriage in whatever style feels comfortable to them. We need to establish broader views of what constitutes a family. My son and I are a family. Our family also consists of my parents, my brother and his family, aunts and uncles and cousins, and our many friends. They all provide us with nurturing and a feeling that we belong together.

Yes, in some families it is possible that co-parents are playing out their need to continue fighting. Certainly in other families this is not the case.

I have spoken with many co-parents; while they all do not get along without difficulties, and some have their differences, they generally feel good about each other as people and as parents. I do remember times when Jeff and I had trouble getting through our business because we each seemed to have hidden agendas. Mine had to do with making Jeff feel guilty and his had to do with reacting to my guilt-inducing behavior and fighting to maintain his parental equality. So we definitely had our struggles. Now, after nearly four years of co-parenting, we each know what areas are apt to cause us problems. We watch out for potential trouble spots between us. We can, if we need to, conduct our routine business in a matter of minutes, and we usually do our business in a spirit of cooperation and in an atmosphere of comfort and ease.

If co-parenting can mean hidden destructiveness for some couples, it is definitely creative for others. Here is one professional's view of my own family situation, as expressed to me in an interview; Ms. Weinberger says:

I think co-parenting has been enriching to Joshua's life because he's seen all kinds of loving negotiations and communications going on between you and Jeff. You can obviously do that in a family that's unbroken, and I think you're doing it as strongly in a family that is broken. That's something that kids in a visitation situation don't see nearly as much of. They don't get nearly the same sense of example— or model—of what it means to be committed enough to human beings and the process of communication in order to work things out. So I think that's one of the best things about co-parenting. Joshua sees that example and internalizes it, and undoubtedly it means he'll be able to do it himself. It enhances his definition of what love is.

Co-parenting gives individuals more of an opportunity to be independent adults, not less. It is a basic misunderstanding to think that co-parenting forces people to stay locked into a childish relationship with each other, or that it prevents people from being able to make independent life choices. I certainly can choose where I want to live, and I choose to live close to Jeff so that Joshua can have a primary relationship with both of us. I do not choose to be apart from Joshua and I do not choose for Joshua to be apart from his father. That is a decision made out of strength, not weakness. Co-parenting and the child-free time I have have allowed me to make more of a life for myself than any other custodial arrangement would, except perhaps for one where Jeff would have total custody. That, however, would exclude a life for myself as an active, involved parent.

In an article called "The Best of Both Parents," published recently in the *New York Times Magazine*, Charlotte Baum (co-parent of three children) responds to the professionals' view of dependency between ex-spouses in a co-parenting situation: "Some psychologists cautioned us that the frequent contact our situation demands would be a way for us to avoid making a complete break and to continue a husband-wife dependence that in their eyes was illegitimate. The argument still puzzles me because I wonder how we could sever our ties with each other when we have children in common who will remain a constant in our lives. Our dependency on each other, if that is the proper term, is centered on the children. We do not turn to each other for comfort when we have personal problems. We do rely upon each other to take over in some situations, to help out when the children are involved. . . . Joint custody doesn't create an artificial bond; children link you forever."

Psychologists and social workers who dismiss shared custody as a viable method of child raising are also among those who simply do not believe in the concept of a "friendly divorce." Those who accept the idea of sharing custody, on the other hand, realize that friendly divorce is more than an academic concept. It is a way of living which means that, given the fact that a couple is divorced, the children of that couple are provided for, cared for, and loved by the two people who care about them and love them the most.

The opinions I have presented of professionals in the mental health field who are opposed to co-parenting are not based on documented evidence. Rather, these are opinions about custody and child raising that are based on custom and ideology and that have been solidified over the years. But "the mere fact that we have a custody tradition in America," write Susan Gettleman and Janet Markowitz in *The Courage to*

Divorce, "does not mean that it is a rational or healthy tradition." There is a belief system which says that after separation or divorce a child needs one home. I have another belief system which says that a child *can* feel good about himself living in two homes. Neither view can be supported by concrete proof. The evidence I have in favor of co-parenting exists in the form of my son and other children I have met who feel lucky to have such loving relationships with both parents and who have adjusted well to their new living arrangements. At this point, that is all we have to go on, and it is enough for me to continue.

Like the vast majority of professionals in mental health fields, members of the legal profession are generally resistant to the idea of co-parenting. Lawyers and judges too are influenced by the social climate which, for the last 50 years or so, has supported the practice of awarding custody to the mother. Previously, fathers always got custody of their children. Around the turn of the century, it became more common for women to be left with the care of the children, as fathers went out to work. Psychological theorists of the early 20th century looked to mothers as the more natural caretakers of the young. The "tender years doctrine" held that young children were better off in the care of their mothers.

Now, however, more and more divorced mothers are out in the work force (working outside the home) more and more fathers are claiming their legal right to the custody of their children. There is no good reason to believe that men cannot be nurturers and caretakers of the young.

Throughout the country, courts are beginning to recognize joint custody as a legal entity. As of January, 1978, reports *Newsweek,* "fifteen states have passed parental-equalizing statutes holding that both parents are to be judged on an equal basis in determining the custody of the child." *Women in Transition: A Feminist Handbook on Separation and Divorce* (1975) states: "It seems that some important changes are being made today, but it may still be too early to tell just how real these changes are. The present trend seems to be away from assuming that either party has a *right* to custody and toward looking at the total family situation and figuring out what would be best for the children. Some courts are trying to develop some guidelines for how this decision is made while in others it depends entirely on the feelings and prejudices of a single judge."

Many lawyers feel that joint custody may be a fine idea, but that it presents practical problems—including major problems for the lawyer. Generally lawyers seek to convince their clients who ask for joint custody that the best arrangement is full custody. Joint custody definitely is an inconvenience for lawyers to work out. It is not so clearly defined as the arrangement in which one parent has full custody. Moreover, any idea of shared custody is in direct contrast with established divorce law, which is based on what is essentially an adversary system. Co-parenting, or joint custody, is a cooperative venture on the part of both parents.

Most lawyers will tell you that it is best to keep a custody decision out of court. The courts are the arena of last resort and only if the parents and their lawyers cannot arrive at a mutually satisfying custody arrangement will the court impose a solution. On the other hand, some parents have reported that prior to going to a lawyer they had already agreed on joint custody, only to find that their lawyers were not willing to go along with this agreement. Marcia Holly, in an article on joint custody which appeared in *Ms.* magazine, states: "There have been legal problems. My former husband and I waged a more difficult battle with the lawyers than we did with one another; they wanted one or the other parent named as custodian. We were more fortunate with the representative from Family Services who recommended that our daughter reside with me but that we be given joint custody."

Some couples choose to fight for shared custody even though they know it will be difficult. There have been landmark decisions in various states that ensure that no one parent will have full custody, but that it will be shared jointly. Some people feel more comfortable with a legal agreement in hand.

*Before we first went to the lawyer, we had worked out our own ar-
rangement. He resisted us for months about joint custody, thinking it
was unreasonable. Then more and more people went to him, wanting
joint custody, and we forced him to reevaluate the idea until finally he
said it was beginning to make sense to him. Fortunately, we had
clarified our own position about it before we went to see him. As far
as we were concerned, his position had been unreasonable.* [Steve]

Dr. Roman suggests that the courts "begin with a presump-
tion in favor of joint custody and reject this arrangement only
when there is compelling reason to do so." This might be one
solution. Certainly this would help to eliminate the adversary
process of divorce in which ex-spouses and their lawyers wage
battle to settle issues of property and custody.

If you did want a legal agreement which said you had joint
custody of your children, what would that mean? Dan
Molinoff, a lawyer who shares custody of his children with his
ex-wife, points out two major provisions of a co-parenting
agreement in an article written for the *New York Times:* "One
main provision of such an agreement is that the parents are required to consult with each other regarding all matters concerning the education and welfare of the children. In essence, this
means major decisions are arrived at together, just as they
probably would have been had the marriage remained intact.
Another important provision is that children reside legally,
albeit during different periods, with both parents. The effect of
this is that neither parent exercises visitation rights; rather,
both have custodial rights."

The agreement that I live by is the separation agreement that
Jeff and I wrote. This agreement is not presented as a document
to be reproduced. It reflects the spirit of my relationship with
Jeff and our commitment to co-parenting. Our lawyer coun-
seled that any contract between two individuals is a legal contract; however, unlike other legal contracts, settlements concerned with child support, visitation, and custody are never
necessarily final. If our circumstances changed and one of us
wanted to bring a matter into court, it is not clear whether a

court would enforce our agreement. This would be true whether an attorney wrote the agreement our whether we did it ourselves. Our attorney, Ms. Volkman, states, "This is a sample and of course the best interest of the child is always paramount and can alter any private agreement or court order as to the child."

We wrote the first version of our agreement within weeks after we separated, agreed to renegotiate the following year, and then drew up a third version, which remains in effect until now. (A copy of this is shown on pages 101 and 102.) I should say that not much has changed in any of the versions. When we decided to divorce, we did show our agreement to the lawyer (Jeff did not have a lawyer; we went to see my lawyer together). She suggested we add items 6 and 7. Item 6 made sense to each of us. In the event that Jeff should remarry and want to name his new wife his beneficiary, I would have no insurance on Jeff's life any more. Now, though, I own Jeff's life insurance policy and I pay the premiums. That way, I will always have some security for as long as I decide to keep up the payments, and if Jeff wants to take out additional insurance to cover a new wife, he can do that. He, in turn, continues to pay premiums on my life insurance.

The lawyer also suggested that we agree that we each have the right to see each other's pay checks. Jeff and I both felt this was not necessary, since we had been trusting each other and dealing in good faith for two years by then. But the lawyer advised that we cover ourselves on the grounds that you never know what the future might bring, in terms of animosity, other relationships and added financial responsibility, and so on. We agreed to it—although I still feel it was pretty much for the lawyer's sake.

I want to mention something about Item 4. Jeff and I each have professions, though at various times we have talked about not working at them for a while. There was a time when I was on unemployment, and I saw this as a luxury on my part. As I might have gotten a job which would have paid me quite a bit more money, there was no reason for Jeff to assume more

FINANCIAL AND CUSTODY AGREEMENT FOR MIRIAM AND JEFFRY GALPER

effective 3/1/76

Custody of Joshua:

We agree that we will have joint custody of Joshua. Who he lives with at what times will be jointly determined by us as we see fit. This includes vacation times, holidays, regular weekly schedule, and summers.

Financial agreement:

1. There will be no support paid by either person to the other. Joshua's costs will be arranged for in the following manner: Each of us will pay Joshua's costs, as they arise, for his food, shelter, entertainment, daily transportation, vacations taken with each of us, and any other regular costs that come up when he is living with that parent.

2. Other costs for Joshua, as listed, will be paid for by both of us in ratio to our base earnings (see below). These are:

   (a) Doctors (including dental, psychiatric, medicines, hospitalization, Joshua's medical insurance)

   (b) Joshua's after school baby sitter (budgeted at $45.00 per month as of this time)

   (c) Joshua's camp, special trips

   (d) school, tutorials, other lessons

   (e) clothes

   (f) big toys (bikes, etc.)

   (g) college

   (h) allowance

We will each keep a record of our expenses on these items, share them with each other to arrive at who owes what to whom, each month, within the first five days of the business month.

3. Our base earnings mean the basic earnings each has on his/her job. Does not include extra earnings from one shot consultations, book royalties, extra research jobs, and so on. We realize that this could be confusing if one or both of us makes a living from a combination of these odds and ends, but we will try to agree fairly and with good will what constitutes our regular earnings and what constitutes extras.

4. If any one of us earns so little that he/she would have to pay less than 30% of Joshua's costs, she/he has to pay that 30% anyway.

5. At whatever point we sell our stocks, bonds, mutual stocks, we split the proceeds equally.

6. We agree to take control and payment of the other person's life insurance.

7. Each of us has the right to see the other's paycheck upon request.

Dated: September, 1976

Signed: _____
      Jeffry Galper

_____
      Miriam Galper

Witnessed: _____

financial responsibility for Joshua's costs—and every reason for me to assume a basic level of care for him, no matter what my earnings. I am prepared, too, to cover any decision Jeff might make in this regard in the same way. Should he decide not to work for a while, he will still have to pay 30% of Joshua's costs, even though his earnings might be considerably less than that.

I think the rest is self-explanatory.

It was not difficult to come to this agreement. Jeff and I shared the basic philosophy that we would each take care of Joshua emotionally and financially.

Legally, I have custody of Joshua. This proved necessary in order for Jeff and me to be granted a divorce in the conservative county where we lived. It didn't matter to us what the law said we could or could not do. Although the law sees me as the legal custodian of Joshua, Jeff and I see it differently, as the first sentence of our agreement indicates. It is because of our basic trust in each other that we were able to determine our own co-parenting arrangement.

Following (pp. 104–105) is a copy of another separation agreement, written by a couple I know with the help of an attorney. Two especially interesting points are that (1) it is stated at what age the children can decide where they will live, and (2) a method of settling any disputes which may arise is provided for.

If you want to write your own separation agreement, I suggest that you read the section (p. 152) devoted to this topic in *Women In Transition: A Feminist Handbook on Separation and Divorce.* There is a copy of a sample separation agreement, as well as suggestions on how to write your own.

My feeling is that unless the courts move to a more open stance about joint custody and co-parenting in general, parents will be pushed still further into adversary positions. This would surely not be in the best interests of the child. Some courts are, however, clearly becoming more open-minded about custody matters.

What happened to us was that we both were suing for full custody. The court ordered the Family Relations Court to make a study and

Co-Parenting

Preliminary Draft of
An AGREEMENT OF SEPARATION
Between Alice and Bertrand Jarry
10 April 1974

I CUSTODY OF DAVID AND PETER TO BE SHARED

1. Bertrand to have the children for four (4) days and five (5) nights each week, specifically, Sunday through Wednesday days and Saturday through Wednesday nights; Alice to have the children the remaining three (3) days and two (2) nights.

Except that, once a month, for one week mutually agreed on from time to time, Alice will have the children for five (5) days and four (4) nights, specifically, Monday through Friday days and Monday through Thursday nights; Bertrand to have the children on such weeks for the remaining two (2) days and three (3) nights.

2. This specification of shared custody is not to be understood as preventing Alice and Bertrand from entering into mutual agreements for either parent to have the children for longer periods of time, such as vacations.

3. The children are not to be separated from each other for periods of longer than two (2) weeks, unless mutually agreed upon by Alice and Bertrand prior to any actual separation of the children from each other.

II SUPPORT OF THE CHILDREN

1. Each parent will be responsible individually for the financial support of the children during the times in which he or she has custody.

2. The parents will be jointly responsible for providing the clothing and medical needs of the children.

3. Bertrand will not be responsible for the support of Alice.

III CHILDREN NOT BOUND BY AGREEMENT AFTER AGE 15 (Tentative)

Each child may decide for himself, without regard to Parts I and II of this agreement, with whom he will live when he is fifteen (15) years of age.

IV INTELLECTUAL AND SPIRITUAL WELFARE OF THE CHILDREN (Tent.)

1. The education of both children will be at institutions mutually

104

agreed on by both parents. The parents will meet at least four (4) times each year to discuss ways and means of appropriate eduaction.

In the thirty (30) day period immediately following the sixth anniversary of this agreement the parents will discuss and make a financially secure and binding arrangement for the educational future of the children.

2. Spiritual training: To be considered at any later, mutually agreed upon, date.

V DISPOSITION OF PROPERTIES, now held as Tenants by the Entireties

1. The farm which is located in Williamburg Township, Clark County, Missouri, will be maintained as a partnership between Alice and Bertrand, its responsibilities and benefits to be shared equally.

2. The house and property located at 42 Blackberry Drive, St. Louis, Missouri, will be solely owned and managed by Bertrand, who will have the responsibility for its maintenance and mortgage.

VI METHOD OF ARBITRATING DISPUTES (Tentative)

A council of five (5) persons, all mutually agreed to, will be selected; two (2) persons to be nominated each by Alice and Bertrand, and one person to be jointly nominated. This council will act to settle any dispute in the terms of this agreement upon the request of either Alice or Bertrand, and render a binding decision on it.

VII EFFECT OF POSSIBLE FUTURE DECREE OF DIVORCE TO BE NULL

This agreement is made with the understanding that if at any future time there should be made a decree of divorce between Alice and Bertrand, such a decree would have no effect on the intention and actual provisions of this agreement.

_____   _____
(Alice Jarry)   (Bertrand Jarry)

                                                   _____
April 18, 1974   (Witness)

they recommended joint custody. That was the first time we had ever even thought about that.[George]

Attitudes about child rearing change to reflect changing times. Think about how many times Dr. Spock has revised his book, especially the sections that deal with the psychological problems of children and how to deal with them. An edition which was my Bible said that if I wanted to go back to work after my child was born, I should discuss it with my social worker. He doesn't say that now. Too many women have gone back to work, have not discussed it with their social worker (assuming they had one), and their children are fine.

This is a time when professional opinion is still reeling from the effects of masses of children being affected by separation and divorce. It is a time when some professionals in the mental health field have come to feel that the trauma of divorce to children can be minimized. Yet they feel that the only way children can be saved from permanent emotional damage is if they live with their mothers after separation and have some, but minimal, involvement with their fathers. Other professionals, myself included, believe in alternatives to the more traditional forms of custody arrangements; we recognize that there are ways to enhance a child's emotional well-being and contribute to his ongoing involvement with both parents.

My therapist likes co-parenting because she's seen what it has done for me and my family. She has seen the benefits of co-parenting in a real life situation, not in an academic, intellectualized setting. She sees something in real life that works, and she appreciates it. If my therapist didn't support me in co-parenting, it wouldn't create a problem for me. I'd consider that her problem.[Harry]

Professionals with this attitude are in the minority, however. Most professionals speak of negative effects of co-parenting (those discussed at the beginning of this chapter). It is especially difficult to ignore such remarks because, for the most part, they are telling us that our system is unworkable and not in the children's best interests.

What do we do? Use common sense. If you want support and advice and encouragement in your decision to co-parent, look for people who are also co-parenting and have had some practical experience with it. If you feel you need therapy, try to choose a therapist who will support your decision to co-parent, not undermine it.

I went to see a psychiatrist because I was very depressed after my husband and I separated. We had agreed to a co-parenting arrangement, which was working out okay. The children were adjusting to the new routine pretty well, but I wasn't adjusting well to being separated. Turns out the main thing my therapist talked about was that I should change our custody arrangements. He really thought it was weird the way my husband and I had worked it out, and he kept telling me so. I was so confused I didn't know what to do. [Brenda]

If you want a lawyer who will not stand in the way of your decision to have joint custody, do some research beforehand. Ask questions of people, call a local women's center for a referral to a lawyer who would be supportive of your decision. It is possible to work things out in a way that best meets your needs and those of your children, although it may require some extra work on your part.

My lawyer told me that we could keep the separation agreement that John and I drew up by ourselves. She said it was the same as a private contract, and she advised us not to take it through the courts. [Jerilyn]

At the same time that we need support and encouragement in our lives to co-parent, we need to share our experiences with other people. That is a large part of what this book has been about for me. Previously, I had not talked so much about co-parenting, but had rather seen it just as the way I live—nothing extraordinary. What I see now is that if I want continued support and encouragement, I am going to have to educate people about co-parenting. I need to let professionals with whom I come in contact know that I do not categorically accept their opinions. I will listen to their considerations and really hear them. Then I will encourage them to open themselves to considering alternatives to their positions, based on my own experiences.

You do not have to ignore totally what the professionals say about co-parenting. Listen and read, digest what is said, consider if it makes sense to you, and use the information accordingly. But don't forget to look at your children—they will tell you the most about whether or not your system is working.

Books and Articles Cited in this Chapter

Atkin, Edith and Estelle Rubin. *Part-Time Father.* New York: New American Library, 1976.

Baum, Charlotte. "The Best of Both Parents." *New York Times Magazine,* October 31, 1976.

Gettleman, Susan and Janet Markowitz. *The Courage to Divorce.* New York: Ballantine Books, 1974.

Goldstein, Joseph, Anna Freud, and Albert Solnit. *Beyond the Best Interests of the Child.* New York: The Free Press, 1973.

Holly, Marcia. "Joint Custody: The New Haven Plan." *Ms.,* September, 1976.

Molinoff, Dan. "Joint Custody: Victory for All?" *New York Times,* March 6, 1977.

Newsweek, January 16, 1978, p. 54.

Roman, Melvin. "The Disposable Parent." Paper presented at the Association of Family Conciliation Courts, Minneapolis, Minn., May 11–14, 1977.

Women In Transition: A Feminist Handbook on Separation and Divorce. New York: Charles Scribners Sons, 1975.

Facing the Difficulties

> *Of course there are difficulties. But then, there are difficulties in plain old parenting, and there are difficulties in any divorce situation. Whatever the difficulties are, they are manageable, and they are no greater or worse or harder to deal with than the problems any parents face.*
>
> Jeff Galper

When you decide to co-parent, you agree to pursue what is now seen as an unconventional arrangement. Following a course that is unusual may cause you some anxiety; initially you will have to confront not only your own doubts about the soundness of your parenting arrangement, but also those of your family, friends, and community. To be sure, many people will have a negative reaction to your new way of child rearing. And though you may not ask for the opinions of others, you will hear them all the same. You will hear their concerns, misgivings, and apprehensions about co-parenting.

The following kinds of questions and comments are heard often by people who are co-parenting:

—That must be very hard on your child.
—She must be very confused.
—Don't you miss him on the days that you don't see him?
—A child needs one home, not two.
—How does she know where she's supposed to be?

And on and on. These are comments you might hear from people you barely know. It is hard to respond to them. Although you might feel like educating others about co-parenting and widening their horizons a bit, you wonder about the chances of changing their attitudes at all. At these times it is important to remember that most people are not informed on the subject and that they have certain points of view because they have not thought of any possible alternatives.

A further problem is that you are also seen as suspect, denying what's real, if you say, "No, my child is not confused." My friend Barbara M. is often asked how in the world her seven-year-old son could possibly keep straight the arrangement she and her ex-husband have worked out, for they have a schedule which appears confusing to some people. "He just knows, that's all," is her answer. Her seven year old, also named Joshua, has never had any trouble remembering where he is supposed to be on any day of the week. This is not easy for many adults to accept, so it can cause difficulties for us in relating to some individuals outside of the co-parenting world.

As part of this outside world, your children's school teachers may also be reluctant to accept your co-parenting arrangement. To many of them co-parenting is a new, possibly not a very good, idea. Joshua's teachers have not liked our arrangement at all, and they have told us so. Jeff and I realize that it is important for us—the only co-parents in our community that I know about—to talk more with Joshua's teachers and communicate more about what co-parenting is like for our son.

We've had two experiences with teachers, one positive and one negative. Margaret's first-grade teacher was very understanding of our needs as co-parents. She made sure that school announcements were sent to both of us, she knew Margaret's schedule, and she was very aware of our situation. It made going to parent-teacher conferences a real pleasure for me and Kate.

The second-grade teacher was not at all accepting of Margaret's living arrangements. One time she asked the kids to draw pictures of their families and Margaret started drawing two different houses with us and our new assorted family members in each house. When she got negative feedback from the teacher about the picture, she changed it totally. She drew a picture of me and Kate with herself in the middle holding hands with each of us; there was a house, one house, in the background with smoke rings coming out of the chimney. She figured out what the teacher wanted, and she did it. Of course, it had no relationship at all to Margaret's reality. [George]

It is true that many people who are unfamiliar with the details of how co-parenting works tend to feel intimidated, uncomfortable, or puzzled by it. In general, new ideas about raising children seem to arouse opposition. It is hard for some people to understand what co-parenting is about if they are not close to the situation. Others may be upset by the idea of co-parenting because it threatens their ideas of what successful parenting looks like. Thus if an unhappily married couple is staying together "for the sake of the child," for example, they would *need* to see the option of co-parenting as unworkable— for if they accepted the feasibility of co-parenting, they would then have to question their own assumptions and examine the reasons why they are really staying together. It might be easier, then, simply to dismiss co-parenting as an effective model after separation and divorce.

At times I am aware that people are watching Joshua very closely—watching him specifically for negative effects of co-parenting. Apparently some folks assume that Joshua will have special problems as he grows up and they are watching him for signs of this. No one can pinpoint what those special problems are, yet the assumption is that they will be there. In addition, people observe the interactions between Joshua, Jeff, and me without necessarily being critical of us. They are interested in our so-called experiment, in our small version of the Brave New World, and sometimes that feels all right with me. But sometimes it feels uncomfortable. Perhaps it's the curiosity factor that offends me. I know that because co-parenting is innovative people are curious about it; it's just that I'd rather not be the object of that curiosity, or have my son be that object either.

Joshua, on the other hand, seems to be oblivious to people's scrutiny of us. He does not experience this as a problem of co-parenting. Indeed, it is important to distinguish between the challenges co-parenting presents and the problems children have with it. As far as Joshua is concerned, he is just living his life, having fun most of the time, being upset sometimes, doing whatever it is that kids his age do.

Close family members, as well as friends, have reactions to co-parenting that may cause difficulties for us. Women who co-parent often feel as if they are being criticized for not being proper mothers if they are willing to "let" their ex-husbands "have" the children for a few days a week. The assumption, of course, is that the children are hers to give. What kind of mother would agree to be without her children for three days every week? Surely there is something strange about her. Men, on the other hand, are often dismissed as not being the "real parent." A man's role is just not taken that seriously, even if he shares all responsibility for child raising with his ex-wife. In this view of people, men are seen as rather strange themselves. What kind of man would choose to do "women's work?"

My mother-in-law was dead set against co-parenting at first. Now she sees that I'm home a great deal of the time, and she's envious. No one was home with her, and her husband didn't participate in raising their kids. I think the older generation is admiring but they're not quite sure what the cost of it is. A lot of it is in their attitudes about men: "If you're a real man you'd be out there earning a living and if you're sharing custody it means you're not quite fully responsible in some ways." Yet there's an admiration at the same time—something about it must be tough to be a man, doing a woman's work.[Evan]

In the beginning months of our co-parenting arrangement, my parents had difficulty adjusting to the situation. My mother felt that Joshua should be with me all the time. She would get upset when I would say that I didn't want to be with him all the time. She had trouble understanding that I didn't have the total freedom to come to her house for a weekend with Joshua at a moment's notice. I needed to plan such a trip with Jeff in advance, and yet she didn't feel that Jeff's days with Joshua were important for me to consider. Over the years, as my parents have seen my unwillingness, or even inability, to have Joshua for full weekends without making prior arrangements with Jeff, the pressure I have felt from them to do this has decreased. For them it has meant that they do not have constant access to Joshua, since they choose not to relate to Jeff. They too have had to learn what Joshua's schedule is and where they will be able to find him on which days.

I asked my mother what she thought of co-parenting now and this was her reply:

Today's children seem to have the remarkable facility of rolling with the punches and adjusting to crazy situations. Where genuine love and interest in Joshua is evident, he seems to accept almost any arrangement and not suffer any apparent ill effects. But I can't help wishing he led a less complicated life, uncluttered by the need for endless arrangements. Joshua is a delightful seven-year-old child to have around—bright, loving, and articulate. When he is with us, on infrequent but wonderful visits, we love him to pieces, but our pain is there and we worry. What grandparents wouldn't?

Another grandmother I know expressed these thoughts about co-parenting:

When my son and daughter-in-law first told me of their separation, I was crestfallen—but my first concern was for my darling six-year-old granddaughter.

Then about the time I felt I was adjusting to their separation, they hit me with another mind blower! They were going to have joint custody, or do co-parenting, both of which were new terms to me. My son explained that my granddaughter would live with him for half the week and with her mother for the other half. Well, I hit the ceiling! I ranted and raved and said it would be terrible for our granddaughter—being split up like that. She would have no feeling of roots. We argued about it, but they stood firm. My husband and I were heartbroken. We didn't believe it could work.

But I am pleased to say we were wrong.

It's been seven months now and we see positive things happening. Because of their new arrangement, our son and his daughter have become closer to each other than when they all lived together. He really has to take full charge in the absence of her mother. Also, seeing each parent alone has given the child the opportunity to know them as individuals, not just as a parental unit. [Zelda]

In general, concerning the criticisms of co-parenting from friends and family, I find that the surer and more secure I am about co-parenting, the less vulnerable I feel. I don't open myself up for criticism as much. People still question me about co-parenting, still voice negative opinions about it, but I am continually more confident that these opinions belong to them, not to me.

Although I am basically secure with our arrangement, at times the co-parenting way of life can seem absolutely crazy. The feeling of craziness is apt to come with switch times: no sooner have you and your child readjusted to being with each other when he is off for his time with the other parent. Co-parents are constantly adjusting to being with their child again after an absence of a few days, and then saying goodbye for a few more days.

The kids need readjustment time each weekend right after the transition from Lou's home to mine. It seems like I have to lay down the law every week and bang a few heads to make sure that they remember what they can and can't get away with at my house. Sometimes that process can be quite trying. [Gloria]

Picture this scene. Labor Day comes around again. You have been on vacation by yourself for two weeks. Your children have been with their other parent for two weeks. You come home, eager to see them. Switch time finally arrives, you greet your children with much hugging and kissing, and then you and your children proceed to have an awful time together for the next two days. You argue with each other, get on each other's nerves, find each other totally obnoxious to be with, and wonder what in the world you were looking forward to when you wanted to see them again. (It was during a time like this that I decided that co-parenting was the worst idea anyone ever thought of, the worst scheme I had ever participated in. I decided that a person should be with her children either all the time or never.)

Okay, you finally ease into being with each other, although after two days of annoyance you can hardly call it easing in. School will be starting in another day, and you spend some good times gearing up for that. You buy some new clothes, school supplies, a special pad, maybe a new lunchbox, talk about new teachers, and who will be in what class. You feel proud of your baby entering third grade, and you can hardly believe how quickly the years have gone by. Now, it has taken awhile to adjust to being together again after a two week absence, and it feels as though the irritations of the last few days have ended. The intimacy that you're feeling with your child now was worth the hard times of a few days ago.

The opening day of school happens to be a Thursday. Your child has actually taken a bath and washed his hair the night before, looks smashing, all bright and shiny, and is happy to be the first one out at the bus stop a full half hour before the bus is expected to arrive. It is an exciting morning. Soon the other kids begin to come along, their parents are out, and you all wait together (with butterflies) for the bus. Finally, your child goes off to school. Because it's Thursday—which is your particular switch day—you won't see him again until Sunday morning.

That seems like an incredibly long time to wait to find out how the opening day of school was. (Of course I could call Joshua at Jeff's house on Thursday night to find out how things went that first day, and that is what I did. But it's just not the same as being with him on that afternoon.)

115

School only opens once a year, but there are all kinds of occasions which feel like this. So it is difficult to have these constant separations.

I really resent joint custody when, after three days, Aaron goes off. I would like to have a child all by myself and share him with no one.[Evan]

The reverse of this pattern occurs when Joshua and I have been together for an unusually long time. If Jeff goes away, whether on business or vacation, Joshua and I might spend a full ten days together. During such periods we get to know each other's rhythms and moods very well and have what feels like exceedingly intimate times together. More than that, it feels good to know what it is like to be with my child regularly. The hard part is that we have to separate when Jeff returns. Sometimes that feels okay and sometimes it feels just awful. There's nothing more I can say about that.

The first day of the week that I don't have Haika, very often I'll get suddenly depressed or I'll go visit a friend who has kids and spend some time with them, just to be around kids. I feel as though all of a sudden there is a tremendous loss and change.[Steve]

Another problem area has to do with the subject of moving. Indeed, the very word may bring up a rash of anxious questions for individuals who are co-parenting. What if one parent wants to move? What happens then? Do you move and discuss long distance co-parenting? Who is with the children for the school year and who is with them for vacation times? Does it still feel like co-parenting? And what if you know you need to move and want to take the children with you but your ex-spouse definitely wants them to remain with him or her? Does a major custody fight ensue? How on earth do you decide what to do?

For many couples, they decide by deciding to stay put.

I don't think about moving. I'll be here until my son goes off to college and so will my ex-husband. It's important enough to me to co-parent that I would not leave the area. I'm not talking about my entire life, but a period in it. When my son is ready for college, I'll be only 44. That seems real young to me now. [Barbara M.]

This is not a sacrificial attitude. Barbara feels that it is in her best interests, as well as her son's, for her to stay put—even though she knows that some couples do manage effective co-parenting over long distances.

Soon after we separated, Jeff was offered a job in Ottawa. He fantasized about what if would mean if we both moved there. We talked about my looking for a job in Ottawa and taking up separate residences. It seemed like an absurd situation to me, one that would cause greater problems since we would be thrown together more, away from our separate friends, at a time when we were still separating from each other emotionally. This job offer gave us both the opportunity to see how difficult it would be for one or both of us to move, and so it canceled any thoughts we had about moving.

For this period of my life, I am in Philadelphia. Life always has some givens and this is one for me. Yes, I would like other freedoms, but I choose rather to be involved with Joshua's childhood in an active, ongoing way. [Jeff]

At this point, Jeff and I are both committed to co-parenting, to our close relationships with Joshua, and are not considering moving from the area. We now have an understanding that the parent who leaves our area would also be leaving active parenting of Joshua; the parent who stays would stay here with Joshua.

We are at this time, however, each considering moving to another part of the city. This poses questions for us. Should we work toward moving as close together as possible, for the sake of continued ease in co-parenting? Living within a few blocks of each other in the city seems much closer than living within a few minutes of each other by car in the suburbs. We would probably bump into each other much more in the city, since we

117

would be walking more. Is that a good idea? Should we make a concerted effort to move into different neighborhoods for the sake of more space between us, even if it would mean more disruptions for us as co-parents? Should we even discuss it all, or should we each do what we want to do without planning it all out? And how might such a move affect Joshua? Whatever happens, it is important to remember that children are flexible—and I want to think that Joshua will be able to flex with our living in different parts of the city. This may, however, make picking up his boots on a snowy morning a little trickier.

My friend Carolyn is not at all sure that she wants to continue living in the same city that her daughter and her daughter's father now live in. She says:

I just don't want to even think about moving. But it's probably going to happen sometime that we will live in different cities. Ian, Jessie's father, seems very committed to staying in Milwaukee, as is Sara, the woman he lives with, as is her ex. Now there's a man I'm very close to who doesn't live in Milwaukee, and I may at some point decide that I want to live with him. So I always assumed that Jessie had a quote unquote better situation with Ian and that she would be with him most of the time. I don't make that assumption any more. She and I are very close and I just don't know.

What if you and your ex-spouse remain in the same area but your child decides he's tired of switching houses and that he wants to live with one parent all the time? I used to worry about this quite often since I assumed that if Joshua chose one parent to live with, it would be Jeff. I spent a considerable amount of energy feeling badly about this, feeling rejected by Joshua and feeling that I had lost, or would lose, in the battle of the chosen parent. My intellect now says that where Joshua lives doesn't matter. I will always be his mother, he will always be my son, and the love we have for each other will exist no matter where we all live. Emotionally, of course, it will be difficult if or when he chooses to live with Jeff, but I'm just not worrying about it now anymore.

I worry that when Rachael reaches puberty she'll decide to live with her father. That's a tense time anyway between mother and daughter, and then, that's a time when kids look at things through different eyes. Her father has a big house and a lot more money than I have. When she gets to be a teenager she may be more attracted to that way of life. My concern is that I don't think co-parenting is a thing that's going to last forever.[Marilynn]

What if your children have been living in two homes for a number of years now, and the older child, for example, decides this system doesn't work for him any longer. He wants to live in one home permanently in order to have a more regular social life. Your younger child is still content to switch homes weekly. What do you do? I would suggest you maintain an open mind by being flexible and working out what seems best for all of you at the time. I know of a situation in which one child lives with one parent exclusively and visits regularly with his other parent. This child's brother still moves back and forth between houses. It is possible to make special arrangements for unique situations. The form might change over the years, but the context of sharing responsibility for child raising can remain the same.

Some scheduling difficulties that come up periodically involve holidays, vacations, and special occasions. (I have written in Chapter II about how Jeff and I manage vacations and holidays.) We as co-parents don't need to look upon conflicts that might arise as insurmountable. There are ways to work them out, to accept them as part of the package of co-parenting. For instance, as Joshua gets older, he will go away by himself, without either me or Jeff along with him. This past summer he spent a week out of town with my parents; a problem arose when he returned. Who was to be with him, Jeff or me? There was no precedent for this, and I imagine it will happen more, as he might go away to camp, for instance. Jeff and I both had feelings about wanting to spend a few days with him as soon as he returned, so we talked it over several times until we reached an agreement.

Co-Parenting

The end-of-the-year holiday season can be very anxiety-producing.

Christmas is really the hardest time for us. Both John and I have always felt tremendous strain about the family being split up at Christmas time. We've always managed to make it okay for the kids, but for us it's the worst time to get through. Do you know that every year we've almost gotten back together again at Christmas? We've talked about it every year and it's almost happened. For the past few years, whichever one of us wasn't living in the house would move back in and stay overnight for Christmas—not just for the day, but through the New Year's holiday.

There's really a strong sense of the priority of the family ties, of having the hearth, the warm hearth around which everyone gathers and the sense of being rooted with these people. Around Christmas all those things begin to seem more important than anything else. Even this year I have found myself thinking about getting back together with John already—thinking oh, well, we could get rid of Susan, the woman John lives with, and Paul, my man, and it'd be so much better and what do we think we're trying to do anyway? Why don't we be more realistic and realize that life is not about having these perfect relationships? Life is about raising children, having a stable home, and all those things.

But then I felt that I wouldn't want to be over there for Christmas this year. I don't really feel good in that situation. Yes, we're going to try to split it as we've done on the other holidays, alternating from year to year. One Thanksgiving the kids are with one parent, and one Thanksgiving with the other. And we're going to do that with Christmas, only we're going to try dividing the time so that each of us gets to spend some of Christmas with the children. [Jerilyn]

Ordinary days which deviate from the routine can present a problem too.

When Joshua doesn't have a full day of school, for whatever reason, Jeff and I are usually on the phone about it. Who can be available to Joshua for the afternoon? "Well, I'll call John's mother to see if Joshua can play with him that afternoon. You call the school to arrange for changes in bus dropoffs." We get a notice that we are to meet with Joshua's teacher for a conference at 12:30. That's the worst time of the day for Jeff and me and we need to re-schedule. "When can you make it? Who will call to rearrange the time?"

It's not that such things in themselves are difficult to do. All parents are constantly making such arrangements. In more traditional homes, these tasks usually fall to the mother. Co-parenting assumes that both parents will take responsibility for the child's day-to-day living. That just means a lot of phone calls, a lot of checking back and forth. But the special concern here is that you are in continuous contact with your ex-spouse; you are working to dissolve the spouse system while maintaining the parent system. This can be difficult emotionally for both of you. It can be hard on you to talk to someone fairly often when your feelings toward that person may be unresolved at best.

In time, of course, this situation will get easier for you. It will become absolutely routine to call your ex-spouse and make all the appropriate plans and schedules. It can become a simple business-like operation in which emotions do not run high and in which there is general good feeling between the two of you. Just give yourself time to achieve this level of communication.

Many co-parents report that some of the most awkward situations occur when they begin to form loving relationships with other adults. Their children seem extremely threatened and jealous, and their new mates have difficulty adjusting to the fact that they are involved in intimate relationships with their children. It seems that everyone has strong feelings and the co-parent feels caught in the middle. All separated and divorced parents have to work out these new relationships; but, compared with other individuals in a primary parenting role, the co-parent has more day-to-day time away from the children in which to pursue other relationships. As Jerilyn says,

My children have never had to deal with my having another man around. My social involvements with men have always been on my own time and I never even had a significant relationship where I'd want to bring a man home to the kids. Now, all of a sudden, there's

this big guy around and the children are upset. And the big guy, Paul, he's upset too. He's not used to being around kids and I don't think he understands very well how they work. And then there's me. I guess it's all worth it but sometimes I wonder.

We don't even have words to identify the relationships our children have with significant adults in their lives who are not their parents:

I'm Jessie's father and Carolyn is her mother and you can't mess with that. That's safe and established. But Jessie really didn't know what to call Sara, the woman I live with, and Paul, her son. Sara is definitely not her mother but is clearly a significant person in her life. So she made up the name of the Da Family. Sara is her Da Mom and Paul is her Da brother. It seems to work for her.[Ian]

What happens when one of you forms a relationship with someone who wants to be an active parent to your child? Your child already has two active parents. It's not as if his father sees him occasionally, or is minimally involved in child raising, so that someone else could easily fill that role. If you live together, you will have to integrate that person into your relationship with your child and also into your relationship with your ex-spouse, which are both structured around co-parenting.

Daddy's girlfriend Maria, she sometimes comes over and spends the night, or he goes over to her house and spends the night. But whenever she's here, she's just like a friend to me and my brother. She's friendly and I like her; she's nice. It's not like she's trying to be a mother. She's just being a friend.[Kathy, age 13]

How is your relationship with your ex-spouse affected if this other person has no children of his own and wants the responsibilities of a parent in relation to your child? Do the three of you go to parent-teacher conferences? How would that feel to all of you? This circumstance might best be managed by a three-way discussion. Would you all feel comfortable being at the child's birthday party or school graduation? These are events which all parents or surrogate parents want to be of.

For some parents, the presence of an ex-spouse's new mate at a special occasion is unacceptable. Lois said that she and her ex-husband had planned a big party for their daughter together:

Marvin wanted his girlfriend to come and I was absolutely opposed to that. He was unhappy about it but he went along with my wishes.

My feeling is that there are ways to arrange such things without conflict. It would be fine with me if Barbara (Jeff's girlfriend) wanted to be present at any special event which concerned Joshua. I know that for any kind of occasion we could work out an arrangement acceptable to all of us. There should be room for lots of loving adults in a child's life. I feel the same way about this situation as I do about the issue of toys and clothes. If you perceive it as a difficulty, then it certainly will be one. If you don't see it as a problem, then it need not be. Perhaps you think this is too simplistic. What I've found is that my feelings and my relationships are always easier to manage when I choose to define fewer things as problems or difficulties. I prefer to see these sensitive situations simply *as* sensitive situations that can be worked out with just a little extra care and thoughtfulness on the part of everyone involved.

There's a new man in my life and he wants to be part of my family. He wants to be a father to my daughter and I don't know how that's going to affect my relationship with my ex-husband and Judy's relationship with her father. Judy is feeling a lot of conflict already. Jonathan is a warm, loving person and while Judy's father is very involved with her, he's just not demonstrative at all. So if she likes Jonathan, is she being disloyal to her own father? We've talked about how she can get different things from different people, but I just don't know how it will all work out. [Nancy]

As our children get older, other sensitive areas may present themselves. In general, adolescents don't particularly choose to spend a lot of time with their parents. What of the co-parents of an adolescent who pressure him to spend time with each of them separately? An adolescent may find this situation untenable. An adolescent may just not want to leave one parent's home for another's, especially as a weekend with social events comes up. What happens then to the "schedule" and the principle of equal time? All may just get thrown out the window.

It's hard to envision co-parenting working out as smoothly for an older child as for a younger one. I remember that when we first started it seemed impossible to envision it even for a younger one. It is most likely that the future will bring an easier resolution to these dilemmas than it now seems. When I begin worrying about how a teenager could possibly live happily under these arrangements, I start to think, well, if it doesn't seem to be best then, we can be open and creative about changing things. The problems we now anticipate will not be problems in the way we think. At that point Joshua will have lived this way for ten years plus, and it will just be his way of life, and things will work around that. [Jeff]

It is natural to worry about what the future will bring. Perhaps, though, we can take some comfort in looking at the past and in seeing that things have, in fact, worked out even easier than we anticipated. Wondering how your arrangement will work out over the long haul is one of the costs of doing something for which there are no time-honored rules. When your child has two homes, it is not easy to read a book which says, definitively, that a child needs one home, not two. How do *they* know what your child needs? Well, they're the experts, aren't they? I am coming to believe that they are not the experts. We are. We are the ones who are living in this situation. And while we might not feel it is easy, we feel good about our lives, our relationships with our ex-spouses, and the healthy development of our children.

What is most important to me is that I have a primary role in parenting Eric and this can only happen in a co-parenting arrangement since we are separated and both want a primary role. The advantage for

Eric of co-parenting is that he has a close, active, healthy relationship to both parents and he knows that both parents love him. Neither has abandoned him.[Jim]

When our own anxieties do come up, we need to remember that we are working on building new models of parenting and structuring new ways of relating to our children. Yes, there are difficulties in this model, as there are in any model of child raising. As mothers, we want to maintain an intimate relationship with our children and pursue our own individual, adult interests. Fathers want to assume a more involved relationship with their children and think carefully about what their priorities in life really are.

This is not an easy task. It is challenging to be different, and it is difficult to ask our children to be different too. But the reward is in the extra measure of fulfillment that these differences bring about.

The Long Haul

I often wonder about the future and think a lot about structures and the meaning of life. And in the co-parenting situation there's a brand new structure evolving for how to raise children. Now that's got to make an impact in our world. Our children will be different, but in the long haul who could possibly know what that difference will be?

Roberta Kallan

Co-parenting has evolved out of a broader movement of social change. The women's movement of the late '60s and early '70s created an atmosphere in which the dynamics of male-female relationships were explored and traditional role expectations were questioned.

Women began to challenge the point of view which said that only full-time mothers, mothers who stayed home, were good mothers. They wanted to expand their horizons and define their world as more than one of wifehood and motherhood. Increasing numbers of women were choosing to return to work before their children were teenagers. They wanted more out of life for themselves than merely the fond expectation of getting out of the house at some unspecified time in the future.

What was the impact on men of the changes women were going through? Men began to take more responsibility for child care and household chores. And they were encouraged to be full partners in the tasks of raising a family and running a household. The women, in turn, wanted to share in the economic responsibilities of life.

Thus more and more men have opened themselves to the pleasures of active parenting. As nurturers to their children, they are doing so-called "women's work" and they have been willing to struggle with the changes that this work—and this label—brings about in their lives. They have been willing to reorder their priorities and question some assumptions about the role of a career or a job in their lives. They have felt their need to maintain a sense of family in whatever kind of family structure exists, and they have come to see that being fathers to their children is not incongruous with their manhood.

I know of many married couples who are sharing the responsibilities for raising their children, even on a daily basis; some choose to structure this in a systematic way.

Barry and I decided we could adapt some of the principles of co-parenting to child care within our marriage. We have worked out an arrangement where we know which days we each have primary responsibility for Danny. On the days that Barry is responsible for Danny, I am free to be involved or to bow out; the choice is mine and the arrangement works the same for Barry. Thus, I feel no compulsion to be home the days I do not have primary responsibility because I know Danny is well taken care of. The reality is that I probably spend more good time with Danny than I would have previously because it is time freely given and I know I will also have time to myself at a later time. The arrangement has also eliminated hassles concerning Danny that used to arise between Barry and me.[Alice]

Just as married men have become more involved in parenting, many separated or divorced men find co-parenting a natural extension of their fatherhood.

Men who co-parent have the experience of developing a side of themselves that our usual socialization patterns have tended to inhibit. They talk about discovering a gentle, soft side of themselves that comes from being with their children. The man responding to his child's emotional needs responds out of love and genuine feeling, not out of role fulfillment (as is sometimes the case with women). Men learn they can be emotional caretakers too, and they feel good about their capacity to nurture their children.

A child's love is unconditional. It is pure and unique in that respect. Too many men miss having that experience. It isn't the same as adult love—it isn't what you get or want or need from the love of an adult. It is its own special thing. You can live without it, but it is very, very special to experience it.[Jeff]

Men who have cared for their children when they were married are not willing to give up a close relationship with their children after they are divorced. They have found a way to continue to express this care through co-parenting.

Many men I have talked to have told me that they find their relationship with their children improves through co-parenting. These men, who share the parenting responsibilities with their ex-spouses, note that as soon as they moved out of the house they experience an improvement. For some it's meant getting out of a household that was full of the tension of the deteriorating relationship between the parents. For others, it's meant that they have been able to carve out a space for themselves where they can work out their own rhythms with their children. And for others it has meant becoming secure in their own ability to parent.

American society places a premium on motherhood as the best means for raising children. As a result, most men feel inadequate to the task, and never realize their potentials as fathers, and consequently as rich human beings who are capable of loving and being loved. Being alone with Jessie has meant all these things to me and many more. Now, when I look at Jessie, she seems so happy and in such great shape. I realize that I must be doing something right. I have learned how important I am to Jessie and how important she is to me.[Ian]

Attitudes in our society are changing as a result of the thinking of the human liberation movements. The women's and men's liberation movements have affected not only those people who have been directly involved in them. Women who have never defined themselves as feminists are going back to school and working outside the home. They are becoming more independent people, emotionally as well as financially. Men who do not especially identify with any "new male consciousness" are more accepting of women's interests outside the home. They are participating more and more in their children's daily lives and are getting much pleasure from this kind of involvement.

The attitudes reflected in our everyday events and living dynamics create change in the social system in ways we cannot see fully at present. A father who is involved in his child's schooling is going to create a different pattern of teacher-parent interaction, which will in turn affect teacher-student interaction. A father who tells his work colleagues that he cannot be at an early evening meeting because he has responsibilities for his children on a given night will stimulate their thinking in a new way. They will be forced ot recognize that taking care of the children is of major importance to this father. His voice is in the minority, perhaps, but it is bound to have repercussions. Any announcement of difference will stir people; they might be threatened, surprised, supportive, antagonistic—but there will be some reaction.

There are times when I've said to my colleagues that they shouldn't have meetings between 5:30 and 7:30 P.M. because that's hard on parents. They just assume that anyone can meet at any time and that you have your slave at home to take care of the kids. Or you should get a sitter and it doesn't matter if it's the first day that your kid is coming back to you. The kind of life I'm living doesn't mean that I do less work or qualitatively less good work. It does mean that I have to set things up differently and that I need help in doing that.[Steve]

So co-parenting forces you to interact with the social system in ways that you did not expect. Because you are doing something that is unusual, you find yourself in a position of needing to educate people, talking about what you do and why you do it, and pushing back your own boundaries to take in more of your world.

It is important to look at ways in which people can share their lives and be of assistance to each other. One of these ways is in coming together to work on common problems in our communities. One such effort is being made in New Haven, Connecticut, where about 40 families are co-parenting in a spirit of cooperation. Recently, I visited their community and met with this group of people. They share child care responsibilities and join together to work on common issues related to co-parenting.

This co-parenting community evolved out of the people's work in a parent-run cooperative day care center. As a number of marriages were beginning to break up, they expanded their cooperation around day care to include the new structures they were creating around parenting. These people had also been involved in women's and men's liberation movements; their day care center was one in which mothers and fathers participated equally. Further, they have felt a need to expand their values in other areas of their lives besides their way of child raising. They work toward integrating as much as possible in their lives in order to be most successful in their co-parenting.

Joint custody is not a thing in itself. Other problems will come up unless you establish a prior commitment to making the community change. For some of us in New Haven, we are attempting to solve other problems communally, as well as co-parenting.[Evan]

For instance, they have become a major force in the public school system, working to assure that their interests and their children's interests are being recognized in the school setting.

Following are comments of four people about their involvement with their local school system and the kinds of difficulties they run into:

A lot of us send our kids to the same school. We have a real influence on the school, in the PTA and the school council. In some ways it's good and in some ways we've been co-opted. The only parents who hang around in the morning waiting to see what the teacher is doing with the kids are the people who co-parent. [Geoff]

At the school many of our kids go to, one out of seven kids lives either with just one parent or with two parents separately. The school system needs to respond differently to these children, to set up new structures so that co-parenting is facilitated, even if parents live far apart—say, for one semester to be spent in one school and the next semester in another. [Carol]

School is very awkward in handling co-parenting. Messages get sent to one parent and not the other. They don't nurture the concept of co-parenting at all, no matter how much we've done on the council and elsewhere to foster their recognition of the way a lot of us live. Their structure just grinds along the same old way. [Susan]

Even to register your child at a school he needs two sets of applications—one with his father's address, one with his mother's address, and emergency numbers to call, people to reach, etc. The standard form just wasn't big enough for all the information. [Bruce]

The individuals in the New Haven community of co-parents have become a support group for each other. They meet regularly to share their common problems and work out common solutions. The support group has helped couples who are separating to avoid court fights by mediating and facilitating differences. One couple who were fighting over who got which books and which records was asked to come to a meeting—a jury of their peers—in which they were forced to be civil, reasonable, and fair with each other. This method has not always been successful in settling questions of money and custody, yet it represents an attempt to provide new structures for new times. Many of us for whom marriage has not worked have needed to create our own structures to serve our present situations.

131

The people who live in the co-parenting community have arranged their schedules so that, whenever possible, the children switch homes on the same day. This means that for the children who have a parent living in the same communal house, they will all be at that house together and leave for their other home on the same day. In this way, the children have a large network of friends who live exactly the way they do. These children feel sorry for a kid who does *not* have two homes to live in.

People in New Haven have found that working on their common problems collectively has made their lives much easier, and more fun. Their involvements with each other include more than strictly co-parenting. I do not think that their way is necessarily a model for all of us who are co-parenting. It is, however, a provocative, innovative, exciting model to think about.

Social changes that have come about as a result of recent (and current) liberation movements are still going on. New configurations will emerge, ones that we do not know about now. I hear about more and more separated or divorced couples who want to create new systems, who want alternative custody arrangements. While co-parenting may feel new and unusual now, it will not be surprising to find that a variety of social structures—like the New Haven community—are continually being established.

Where I live in Milwaukee, co-parenting has created through the Children's Discovery Center a strong community awareness, and has shown the potential to establish community support systems that help people break away from some of the isolating effects of traditional family life. Insofar as it points to communal arrangements for parenting, it directs all of us toward new ways of sharing our lives with others.[Ian]

As we look toward the future for new models of family living, we naturally wonder how the present arrangement will be for our children in just a few years. Of course, there is no way for us to know what the future will bring. We can plan for it, but we cannot plan the outcome. As co-parents, we cannot predict what kind of adults our children will be; no parents can.

What are my feelings about the unknown and the future? Well, when Aaron is with his mother I don't know what's happening there, and I've learned to trust that. Thinking about fear, about what's going to happen to the children when they grow up, is fear of the unknown and fear of the time when you no longer have control of every aspect of your kid's life. And I think co-parenting prepares you for that eventuality because you have a regular experience of trusting things that you don't know about, of trusting where you don't know what's going on.[Evan]

For the children, co-parenting can have a very special influence on their upbringing. Indeed, they have more of their parents' individual time and attention than most kids do. They have seen that their parents, while no longer living together, retain a major commitment to parenting and to being available to them in a complete sense. They are likely to experience an expanded range of activities and to have relationships with a greater number of caring adults than they would if they were in a more traditional custody arrangement.

You get to know more people, 'cause your Dad has a lot of friends and your Mom has a lot of friends. Otherwise you would just know who your Dad and your Mom know together. And you get to go more different places than you would if you were one whole family.[Joshua, age 7½]

Children growing up in a co-parenting situation know that many solutions to life's problems and many options are within the realm of possibility. They know that some people may view the way they live as unusual, although to them it feels ordinary to live exactly as they do. Children of co-parents see that it is possible to divorce and not hate an ex-spouse, and they learn to broaden their own horizons as well as their view of adult relationships. They learn at an impressionable age that life is not a matter of either/or choices and black/white issues, but that it is

133

constantly subject to flexibility and all kinds of adjustments. And they learn that people can make choices about their lives and have control over how they live. They seem acutely aware of how things are around them.

The other day someone called; my daughter, who is nine, answered the phone. Someone asked for her mother. She said, "My mother's not here, my parents are divorced, and if you'd like to talk to her, I can give you her phone number." She handled it so smoothly. It was a real clear awareness of the reality, with no emotional connection to that reality. [Geoffrey]

Children whose parents have separated and divorced certainly know that life holds surprises for them and that they are able to adjust to new situations as they arise. Joshua, I feel sure, will be able to deal with the world competently. He has looked back at times that were difficult for him and seen that he has come through well, that he has changed and grown through it all. I know that he feels good about himself.

Jeff and I too have gone through many different phases. While there have been some fairly anxious times for us, we have always been able to be civil to each other regarding Joshua's needs. We have now come to enjoy and appreciate each other in a way that is enriching for both of us. This may have been possible in a traditional custody and visitation arrangement, yet I think co-parenting created the context for these good feelings of ours. We are more to each other than Joshua's parents. We benefit from our dealings with each other in a way that is not only related to Joshua, but is also very clearly related to our liking for each other as people we used to be married to. In this way our lives have been enhanced, and so has Joshua's.

There was a time, not too long ago, when the intact family was seen as the only environment in which to raise emotionally healthy children. In recent years, we have learned not to romanticize the ideal of the nuclear family any longer. We have learned, through our experience, that we can provide emotionally safe environments for our children in various kinds of living situations. Co-parenting, with parents sharing their children equally, is one such kind.

Mothers and fathers want to provide their children with love and warmth, with affection and fun. They also want to live their own lives to the fullest. After separation or divorce, co-parenting provides a dynamic, effective way for that to happen.

An Interview
With My Ex-Husband

JEFF: *I have worked out a lot of problems and I've come to feel good about being a parent. I think that I am a good parent. I do it easily and I get tremendous pleasure from it, and you and I have worked out co-parenting very well.*

MIMI GALPER: The fact that you and I co-parent seems like such a natural part of our lives at this point. It wasn't always that way, though. What memories do you have of your beginning with it?

JEFFRY GALPER: The first period was hard for me. When we separated four years ago, we didn't know anybody who co-parented. In fact, I don't recall that we had even heard of the idea of co-parenting. Our decision to do it developed out of our raw and painful experiences at the time we were separating. For my part, I had just moved out of the house and had strong feelings of having lost a lot of the anchors in my life. Co-parenting didn't mean to me then what it does now. At that time I was fearful of losing Josh. I felt alone in the world anyway. I especially wanted my son with me. At the beginning, co- parenting had a lot to do with my feelings of being painfully isolated from so much that had been my life.

When Josh and I were together, we had close times and good times, although I felt a strong undercurrent of anxiety. I didn't have the idea that we were working out a new model for custody. I felt as though I was struggling to survive, and part of surviving was to stay involved with Joshua.

One of the reasons I feel your book is going to be important to people is that there are many parents who are in the same position that we were in four years ago. Co-parenting is not an option that many separating people have heard of. In fact, I bet many people develop some form of co-parenting as a product of the same painful, unprepared birthing process that we experienced.

MIMI: Do you think it would help them to have heard about the idea ahead of time?

JEFF: Yes, very much so. If people know about this possibility and know that others have tried it and made it work, the whole process might be much easier for them. At a time when people are very upset anyway, they wouldn't have to add to their burdens by feeling as though they were starting from scratch in developing a way to maintain a decent arrangement for parenting.

MIMI: What were some of the ways that co-parenting influenced your life when you first started at it?

JEFF: One of the first ways it influenced me was in the choice I made about a place to live. I wanted to live alone since I had never done that as an adult. I looked for an apartment that would have one bedroom for Josh and one for me and that was also in a good location. The location was quite important to me. I took a place only a quarter of a mile from where we had lived together and where you were still living so that it would be easier to get Joshie back and forth.

I didn't feel confident or relaxed about being alone with Josh at all. So a big consideration for me in choosing a place to live was that there be other kids around. In fact, when I started looking for individual freestanding houses, my fantasy about those houses was that on Saturdays I would be totally alone with Josh with no other kids around. Each weekend I felt as though I had to have companionship for Josh and to have people around for me. The times when I would be alone with him, which in our beginning schedule included all day Saturday, were very forboding. Thursday night and Sunday morning were manageable. Friday night after school to Sunday morning seemed like a really long stretch. It never turned out to be so hard, but my fearful anticipations didn't ease up for quite a while.

As I was saying, my idea in being at the apartment I chose was that there would be lots of other kids around. It turned out there were other kids around, but Joshie didn't get involved with any of them. Still, it was important to me to be there.

MIMI: I remember you were unhappy with the thought of living there and knowing you were doing it because of Josh.

JEFF: I did have feelings, even at that time, though less strongly than now, that I would rather live in the city. But the apartment eventually worked out well for me. That didn't happen, though, until I resolved some of the fears I had. Part of the issue for me was that being a parent did not feel natural.

MIMI: Was that particularly because you were a single parent?

JEFF: Yes, I think so. I had been very involved with Josh when you and I were living together. But it was different from being a parent to him alone. I just hadn't had the same responsibility when we lived as a family.

MIMI: You had constant support.

JEFF: Right. When Josh was born, we knew we didn't know much about being parents. We just started in. But at least there were two of us.

MIMI: Two of us who didn't know anything.

JEFF: Exactly. Parenting alone was different and frightening. For example, at the beginning I would make plans for us far in advance of my time to be with him. On Monday morning, I'd be thinking about the next weekend, and many times I would call people early in the week, perhaps on Tuesday or Wednesday, to set up dates. I don't know exactly what I feared, because when we were alone our time together was fine. It was just the idea that was so upsetting. It took me a long time to change about that. But I came to realize over a long period of time, actually a year or so, that the times that I was afraid of when I was alone with Josh were not as bad as I feared. The worst part was the anticipation of being alone, cut off, just by myself, with a young child. And actually it wasn't easy to become accepted in the world of parents at the apartment. It was mostly a women's world and I didn't fit in too well.

MIMI: They didn't let you in?

JEFF: I wouldn't exactly say I was excluded. But when I talked with somebody about children, our arrangement would eventually come out in the conversation and the easy flow wouldn't be there the way I imagine it is with two women talking together. It just would not click, perhaps because I am a man. Also I was single, and perhaps the mothers were afraid that talking with me would look flirtatious to their husbands. I didn't flirt with the women. I was just friendly and wanted to talk about kids—for example, about where the kids in the neighborhood played.

MIMI: You were seen as a weirdo.

JEFF: My whole situation must have seemed weird to people there. They couldn't be relaxed with me. Nearly everyone that I met who had children was involved in a traditional nuclear family. Still, that apartment was the place where Joshua and I worked out being a twosome, and I feel good when I think back on it.

MIMI: You know, he talks about that place with a lot of fondness. He's mentioned a couple of times, "Oh, that's where my Dad lived at the apartment—" no, that's not what he says—he says, "When *we* lived at the apartment." He'll say the pool in the back had such and such, or I know that kid from when we lived at the apartment. He talks about it with a lot of pride.

JEFF: Josh has gotten good things from each of the places we've lived, though he's less enthusiastic about where we live now. He feels less involved here, as I do, since he knows we will be moving into town and living with Barbara and Ricky by the summer. He feels okay here, but it is not a place that he has dug into. But that is okay with me. I would have been upset about that a few years ago. Now I just don't worry about him so much.

MIMI: Your house is more your relationship with him and his relationship with you, and your relationship is fine wherever you take him. So the physical structure isn't that important to either one of you, in the way that it might have been four years ago. You don't need the externals so much.

JEFF: That's true. And there is also another thing that has changed. Josh can amuse himself much better now than he could three or four years ago.

MIMI: Absolutely. Let's hear it for reading!

JEFF: When I was with him alone in the earlier period, or at least when I fantasized about being alone with him, my idea was that he would be right with me the whole time. Actually, I think that he was with me the whole time. For one thing, I didn't know how to separate from him at the beginning. Also he was more needy at the beginning so that when we were together, we were *really* together. I knew that once I picked him up from school on Thursday, I was not my own man again until Sunday.

That has changed a lot. When I come home, if it is our first day together after being apart, I definitely put time aside to be with him to get well-connected. But it is also most commonly the rule these days that I'll be with him for a while and then move on to other things, like making supper. We have supper together, clean up, and then often I tell him that I am going to be by myself. I just go off and do my own thing. He's around. It is not that I forbid him to be with me. Still, in the time between the end of school and his going to bed, which is about four hours, perhaps I have an hour to myself and then after nine I have more time alone.

MIMI: You would not have done that earlier?

JEFF: No, I wouldn't have done that three or four years ago. I wouldn't have been able to. He would have been too clingy, and I would have been too anxious to enjoy being alone. I think this changed just by practice—just by getting used to it. Eventually I realized that I was carrying around unnecessary anxiety about being with Josh and that being with him was never as difficult as I imagined it would be. Also I experienced much pleasure from parenting. A big part of my reaction to co-parenting was that I myself was frightened a lot for a year or two after we separated.

MIMI: You were dealing with being alone, period.

JEFF: Yes, I was. In fact, that is one area where I confused my feelings and Josh's feelings. I would have very sad fantasies about him feeling isolated in our apartment, about him not having friends, about him feeling lonely for you. It was really me that was having those feelings.

MIMI: So your anxious worries about him were really times of dealing with your anxieties about yourself.

JEFF: That was a big part of it. Part of it also was not knowing things, just not having had enough experience—for example, not having fed him enough so that it could become a casual thing.

MIMI: That was going to be my next question.

JEFF: Yes, I would think about dinners and plan dinners in a fussier way than most people probably do because I wanted him to eat a balanced meal and I wasn't sure how to do that.

MIMI: You wanted to make a balanced meal because you thought he wasn't getting one at my house?

JEFF: Not at all. There was no criticism of you in that. I felt that you would know how to feed him, that somehow it would be easier for you. It was just that I felt that I needed to do the right thing for him.

MIMI: It's not as though you had never cooked before.

JEFF: I had done a lot of cooking. But it was different being completely responsible for Josh. It was a new experience— running a house, being alone, meeting the neighbors on my own, and caring for a child. There were many new things to cope with.

MIMI: What was your worst fear of what would happen?

JEFF: It boiled down to the fantasy that Josh and I would be alone and very isolated, no one to play with, no one to talk with, just by ourselves, and that what we would do is look at each other, and start to cry unconsolably about how alone we were.

MIMI: And *my* fantasy, my worst fear, was that Josh and I would be yelling and screaming at each other when we were alone.

JEFF: Well, it's super-clear. You were working out your anger at me, and I was working out my depression about finally living alone.

MIMI: There you have it.

JEFF: I don't know what you have, but you have it.

MIMI: How about clothes?

JEFF: I had never been involved with organizing or buying Josh's clothes before we separated. When we first separated, I didn't give it much attention. I assumed then that the nicest clothes would be at your house. That's just the way it was. And that came from a general feeling in the beginning that you were more the primary parent than I was. Actually, it is only fairly recently that I've come to *feel* that Josh lives with me just as much as he lives with you.

MIMI: Oh!

JEFF: That was important to me. I realized that about a year ago.

MIMI: What happened?

JEFF: Well, let me describe how I felt at the beginning. I didn't feel deep inside of me that Josh lived as much with me as with you. I still thought that he lived more with you. I was jealous of you and I also did not like that feeling of being jealous. One way in which my feelings came out was in my defensiveness when people would ask, "When is Josh going home?" meaning when was he going back to *your* house. Even though he was with me half the week, the assumption was that when he went to your house, he was going home. I always spoke right up about that. I would correct people and tell them that he wasn't going home, he was going to Mimi's home or to his home with Mimi. But I did feel secretly that his home was more with you and that you were the major parent. I felt that Josh thought your home was more his home also. And yet he knew the idea of our arrangement, which was that it was supposed to be equally shared parenting. He knew he wanted to be with me, so he also supported a fiction, denying that he thought your home was more his home.

MIMI: How did you see him do that?

JEFF: He would say *home* meaning your place, and then he would correct himself and say something like his *Mommy-home* instead. It was hurtful to me that that was the way he felt. Yet I understood that it was so. It has taken a long time for that to shift. Now I feel that it has shifted and I'm glad that it has.

MIMI: You know how I see it shifting? I asked you about the clothes and then you started talking about this. Recently, I think it's less than a year, you have started to buy clothes for Josh that you like, that are nice, that you want kept in your home. You're not telling me not to have those clothes, but you are taking responsibility for the way Josh will look in your home.

JEFF: Yes, that's true.

MIMI: I was surprised by it and taken aback. I would say, "Where did you get those clothes, Josh?" I mean, they weren't even clothes that *I* would buy for him. Not that they were more expensive, but they were stylish and classier. We're not talking about tough-jeans or whatever they are called. They're tight-fitting cords.

JEFF: Well, that was neat for me to remember just now—to acknowledge for myself the shift into feeling like a fully equal parent.

MIMI: What do you think accounts for the shift?

JEFF: Time is a big factor. Even though I acted as a co-parent from the beginning, I hadn't bought completely the idea that I would be a co-parent. It didn't feel completely natural at the beginning to be a parent. As a man, it was not something that I was prepared for. I had some preparation because I was parenting when we were living together. But I didn't have much psychological preparation for being alone with Joshie. I never anticipated what it would be like. It was very new. So having the experience of doing it over a couple of years made it seem familiar and that made a big difference.

I feel too that I now have a solid relationship with Joshie. I understand it. I know what it's about, which I didn't know at the beginning. It's a very firm, real thing.

MIMI: Do you think your relationship with Barbara contributed to this in any way?

JEFF: In a small way only. My relationship with Joshua has been changing right along. We've grown closer and we are more relaxed around each other. It took a while, but it was always moving as I was becoming more comfortable living by myself, was learning more about him and learned that it was easy to be a parent to him. At the same time, as my relationship with Barbara deepened and our lives became more entwined, it did make things easier for me with Josh. I had someone to play with and I felt more joyful.

MIMI: So as you began to feel better about yourself in more areas and to have more competence and experience, you were better in your relationship with Josh.

JEFF: All true. But I've just recalled another big anxiety area! Oh, this one was the worst! Vacations!

MIMI: I know just what you mean!

JEFF: Vacations at the beginning were manic activities for me—the times I spent alone and the times I spent with Joshie. I worried about our first vacation from the minute we separated in February straight through until August. As a result I wound up doing some fabulous things with Joshie and by myself too. But I did it out of tremendous anxiety about what I would do with myself and what I would do with Josh for all that time.

MIMI: How do other people respond to you as a co-parent these days?

144

JEFF: One of the things that I faced and that I still do face is that many people don't fully understand or catch on to our co-parenting arrangement. I feel that at Josh's school, for instance. Oftentimes teachers are not as oriented to me as they are to you. I don't like to be in the position of competing for their attention, although I do let people know that I am fully involved as a parent to Josh. I appreciate your thoughtfulness in keeping me involved when the contacts have been more with you than with me. For example, when a teacher calls you about a problem you always let me know about it.

MIMI: I would never think about not letting you know.

JEFF: I know. It does compensate for the fact that some people at the school and elsewhere don't think of me as Josh's parent as readily as they think of you. Our assumption that things automatically will be shared softens the fact that people out there sometimes don't see me as a parent.

There are some issues that come up at work because of my co-parenting. For instance, since I have been teaching there has been a big increase in the number of night classes, which can mean either 4:00 P.M. to 7:00 P.M., or 7:00 P.M. to 10:00 P.M. I've had some conversations with the person who arranges the schedules for those classes, to let him know my time schedule is tight. He was supportive of me. Still, there have been questions about why I couldn't arrange for a babysitter if I had night classes. Well, of course I could arrange for a babysitter, but I have only half as much time with my son as some other parent would have and I didn't want one night in three automatically shot with a class. I didn't think that was fair to me or to Josh. I arranged the schedule I needed once I had justified that. I had to be aggressive in looking out to protect those evening hours.

MIMI: You know, some people have said to me that it's easier for you because you have a son. If you had a daughter, they say, you wouldn't want to be with her that much. Your identification with Josh is great, and that is why you want to be an active father with him. If you had a girl child, you wouldn't care as much, or it wouldn't be that easy for you to be with her because you couldn't play ball together. And then what would you do? I think that's what the inference is. What do you say to all that?

JEFF: It bothers me when people react that way to me as a co-parent. Different people have all kinds of reasons why they believe it has worked out in this particular case. In one way or another, they all seem to take away from what to me is the most basic fact of the matter. I am my child's parent and I want to be involved with him for the same reasons any parent wants to be, and I've made it my business to see that I am.

In any case, I don't know just how I would react to having a daughter. How could I? I think that fact that my Dad and I had a close relationship predisposed me to be a father who would be involved with his son in a close way. I have the idea that I would be close with a daughter also and that I would be able to get into whatever she was into. Basically, I think it would not be all that different from what Josh is into. Josh isn't a macho kid. He and I don't relate around sports, for example. Having a daughter might seem stranger and I might have to put up with more because people would get more critical of our relationship.

MIMI: Because of questions of sexuality?

JEFF: Yes. I'm aware of sexually tinged interactions that go on with Josh and me, and with a girl it would probably be that much more difficult.

MIMI: On another subject, are there any issues from your point of view about the way we handle money arrangements?

JEFF: Elsewhere in the book you explain how we thought about and organized our money arrangements, and I agree with the things you say there. Basically I feel fine about how we have arranged the whole area. One thing that has come up in conversation between Josh and me is the fact that I earn more money than you do. And it's enough more money to make some difference in the way we live. We have an agreement about money between us that we feel is fair and it does not involve equalizing our incomes as it did when we first separated. We agree on that, but Joshie has feelings about it. It has come up a number of times that I make more money than you do. In fact, we talked about it this summer. We were canoeing on a lake and pretty much out of the blue Joshie said to me, "Dad, how come Mom works more than you do but you have more money that she does?" I felt very guilty and defensive! My first response was, "Josh, Mom doesn't work more than I do!" Obviously I didn't have a persuasive case because I'm at home a day or two a week writing, which is what he sees and there is no way I could convince him that I work as much as you do.

Josh's raising these things brought some issues into my mind, like how I feel about the fact that I can afford to take nicer vacations with him than you can.

MIMI: Have you wondered if that was alright to do?

JEFF: Yes. I felt guilty about it. I feel a little privileged. I can afford some things that you can't afford, and I feel slightly criticized by Josh at times. Maybe he feels that I should equally share all my income with you. Part of my reaction to Joshua is actually my own feeling of self-criticism. I do have some ambivalence about the fact that I earn more than you do.

MIMI: In relation to Josh?

JEFF: Yes, and also I have some lingering feeling about having more than you in general.

MIMI: Well, feel free to make amends!

JEFF: Right.

MIMI: What did you finally say to him this summer?

JEFF: I said that I earn more money than you do because my job pays me more and that's just the way it is. I acknowledged with him that I do make more than you do. Sometimes I get the feeling that he thinks about my financial obligations to you. I wonder if he wonders whether I support you financially and in other ways. In various ways over the years he has checked out my commitment to you and he continues to check that out.

MIMI: How does he do that?

JEFF: When we first separated, he would ask me if I loved you.

MIMI: He never asks me that about you.

JEFF: That was a long time ago. Now, I am remembering something that happened, but I'm not sure if it really happened or not.

MIMI: About Barbara?

JEFF: Yes.

MIMI: You told me one story about him asking did you love me, did you love Barbara, when did you stop loving me, when did you start loving Barbara.

JEFF: That's right. That's what I was trying to remember, but I couldn't remember if I made that up.

MIMI: When he asks you those questions, do you feel defensive?

JEFF: No, I don't. I feel pretty clear most of the time about what is right and wrong for me in relation to you and where I stand about that. I don't feel confused about it. So I feel as though I can present a straight story to Josh and tell him what's what, truthfully.

MIMI: When you and Barbara live together, are you thinking that you will have separate times with Josh?

JEFF: I want to have separate times with Josh, just the two of us. Absolutely!

MIMI: When I think about that, I would see it as such a loss if you didn't. I could see how you would not, just by wanting to be together as a family.

JEFF: It is harder for Josh and me to have alone times now when we're with Barbara and her son Rick. I have been more conscious of that since last summer when Josh expressed some angry feelings about Barbara making me less available to him. Also when Barbara and I live together, it will be easier because a lot of the times with Josh are also my major times with Barb. So when Barb and the kids and I are living together, I'll have more time to be with Barb and then it will be easier just to be alone with Josh and to spend time with Rick also. I am developing an important relationship with Rick and am conscious of wanting to nurture it.

MIMI: We started this conversation with some of your remembrances of your beginnings with the co-parenting arrangements. Would you like to say some things about how you see it now?

JEFF: One thing that I realize I haven't talked about are some of the joys I experience from being a parent. I didn't feel ready at the beginning of our talk. I don't know why.

MIMI: Maybe it's because you had to talk first about the struggles you went through to get where you are now.

JEFF: Perhaps that's why it has come to my mind now. I've talked about a lot of the things that have gone on over the years and have learned some things in the process of talking about them. I saw some patterns and trends and changes. I see how I've worked through a lot of the issues that came up for me about being a single parent and about being a co-parent. Also as we've talked I've thought about other issues that we didn't explore—for instance, other aspects of my relationship with you and my relationship with your parents.

I have worked out a lot of problems and I've come to feel good about being a parent. I think that I am a good parent. I do it easily and I get tremendous pleasure from it, and you and I have worked out co-parenting very well. With all modesty, we are excellent co-parents.

MIMI: Mr. and Ms. Co-Parent!

JEFF: That's us. We have hardly any hassles any more. We give each other support, we both feel confidence that when we're not with Joshie the other one will cover in a way we would approve. We both have free time with complete ease of mind about Joshie. When each of us gets our son back there is absolutely nothing about his having been with the other parent that in any way undermines either of us. In fact, just the opposite. I have confidence that whenever my name comes up in your household you are as supportive of his relationship to me as I am of his relationship to you.

All the problems that I experienced with co-parenting did work out. It's not that I don't have problems now. It's more

149

that things come up from time to time. But my basic stance about Josh is not one of worry or anxiety. Just the opposite. He's just my son, that's all. He's just my son. And just being together is what being his father is about. So I get a lot of pleasure from my relationship with Joshie. And I feel very much love for him and I know that he feels very much love for me. And I love watching him grow up. And I love being part of that.

Appendix

Co-parenting has become much more common since this book was first published, so there are many more of us who can share our experiences and learn from them. I have asked a few of these people to describe their own situations: a lawyer who is a strong advocate of joint custody, several people who are involved in different forms of co-parenting, a man for whom co-parenting was out of question due to archaic laws and an uncooperative ex-wife, and my own favorite ex-wife-in-law. Their stories reveal varied aspects of joint custody—what it takes to make it work, who benefits, the problems involved, and the need for legal reform. What all of them speak to is the inspiring way people have carved out their own paths in broadening their ideas about relationships—the potential and the reality of co-parenting.

CHERYL
Overcoming Your Own Resistance to Co-Parenting

Oliver and I have been co-parenting four-year-old Sybil for almost two years now. We separated in May 1978. We began to co-parent in October 1978, four months later.

During those first four months, Sybil primarily stayed with me. I lived in our large three-bedroom apartment on Broad Street, and Oliver moved to a summer place downtown, and later to Sullivan's Island. During that time, I had much less moving to do and was certainly glad that my nest remained intact. I was pained by our divorce, excited and unsure of the future. I was unwilling to share Sybil equally with Oliver. I feared that if we shared her she would love Oliver more. This fear was my first source of resistance to co-parenting.

While Sybil and Oliver had easy times together, she and I fought more. We also had many loving and intimate moments together. My initial resistance to co-parenting was also due to the separation and losses in my life at that time. Thus I clutched Sybil as a source of stability.

If I had primary responsibility for Sybil, then I knew I would receive child support from Oliver. I was uncertain then that I could be financially self-supporting. Receiving child support from Oliver was, after all, a legitimate way of receiving some sort of monetary remuneration in a customary way. Oliver and I split responsibility for Sybil in a traditional way. I had primary custody of her, while he paid child support. When we agreed four months later to co-parent, we again looked at the issue of money. We could share financial responsibility proportionate to our income or divide her expenses in half. After much discussion, I finally agreed to split Sybil's expenses, with the exception that I wanted to claim her as a deduction on my income tax. Presently, Oliver and I are financially equally responsible for Sybil and each of us declares her as an income tax deduction on alternate years. We also divide equally her preschool tuition and other additional costs. Then I felt Oliver was being petty. Now I know he contributed to my own personal development. Supporting myself financially looked like a fierce monster. Finally, with Oliver's support, I faced the monster directly.

My final resistance to co-parenting surfaced around the issue of Sybil's legal custody. At first, I wanted sole custody of Sybil, to make the decisions in her life. I resisted Oliver's having sole or co-custody. This was my last power play in my relationship with Oliver. If I had sole custody, I would have sole and final decision-making power in issues that involved Sybil. For example, if I wanted to move, I would not have to consult Oliver. I could do just what I wanted to do. Or I could decide what kind of school Sybil went to, without Oliver's approval.

My competition with Oliver continued until we began co-parenting in October of 1978. I did not make the decision legal until the spring of 1979. While I met with my lawyer several times to draw up our separation agreement, he was surprised that I changed my position every few months. As I look back, I am thankful that I experienced my own power-playing and communicated this to Oliver. After much struggle, I realized that I was unwilling to continue a life that was based on competition. What I wanted most with Oliver was a cooperative, loving relationship. We were awarded co-custody.

After my initial four months of resistance to co-parenting, Oliver and I began to share responsibility for Sybil. At that time, we chose to have Sybil shift homes after four days. After a month or two of that schedule, we decided on a weekly schedule. Approximately once a week, Sybil would pack her suitcase with a few favorite clothes and move from my home downtown to her father's Sullivan's Island house. At first, we were fairly rigid about time accounting because we had not developed a cooperative relationship. Nor did we know exactly how to co-parent. Over time, co-parenting has become more flexible because we are becoming more trusting.

Sybil is doing well. She is one of the more fortunate Charlestonians who has a house in town and one on the island. She has her own room in each house, and her own toys in each room. She has different rules in each house, and she appears to discriminate quite well. For example, unless she eats all of her lunch, I don't allow her to eat "junk food." I also don't let her touch my stereo, but she knows that her father will let her play his stereo. She is clear about the differences. The shift between two homes usually occurs at school. She goes to the same pre-school, and most of the transitions are made there. When she moves on the weekend, Oliver and I spend time together so that she sees us together. We have meals at each other's homes, and spend more time together as a "family."

What are the problems? A few months ago, Oliver was offered a year's sabbatical in Texas, a threat to our current co-parenting arrangement. As soon as Oliver was offered the opportunity, he called to see how the move would affect me, him, and Sybil. I was immediately upset and cried. I thought how well our current arrangement was operating and how a move would interfere with it. We started to explore what other solutions we could find, including having Sybil commute by plane every four to six weeks. We also considered having her live with one of us and visit the other for extended periods. None of these solutions seemed as appealing as our present arrangement. Finally, Oliver decided he was unwilling to change his own environment. Similar situations may arise later on, and we would handle them in the same way as any intact family. Neither parent makes a decision without mutual agreement.

I am thankful to have moved through my own immaturity and resistance. I no longer feel stuck, competitive, or angry with Oliver. Rather, our relationship is free, open, and loving. That's because co-parenting needs a cooperative and non-competitive spirit, and the willingness of both parents to be commited to making it work.

Cheryl Keats, M.S.S., is a psychotherapist in private practice living in Charleston, South Carolina.

OLIVER
Making Co-Parenting Work

As I reflect over the two years Cheryl and I have been co-parenting, what stands out most are not the hurt and angry feelings I used to have towards Cheryl, not the disappointment I feel about a failed marriage, but rather the sense of accomplishment that we have been able to put those feelings behind us and make our commitment to be Sybil's parents work. To do that, we both had to deal with our unresolved feelings rather than playing those feelings out through Sybil.

It wasn't easy. There was a temptation to be aggressively "fair" even when fairness wasn't best. For instance, if it was Cheryl's turn to take Sybil but she had an important work commitment, it was easy to say, "tough luck," knowing that the only reason for doing so was to be vengeful. That didn't work at all. On the other hand, if the reverse happened to me, I had to get rid of my feeling of inequity (even though it was fair for me to take Sybil), and accept the hassle of getting Sybil taken care of while I worked. I learned that the world isn't always fair. Taking care of Sybil is not always convenient, and part of making co-parenting work for me was making the commitment to have her any and all the time I could, even when it wasn't easy. It was that commitment which helped me put away my mental ledger book and not worry about whose turn it was to have Sybil or who had her more days in a particular month.

Establishing my own household was mandatory. For me, that was not too hard, but other men I've talked to find this a difficult step sometimes. Laziness is the enemy, and it usually expresses itself in the thought, "It's not fair that I should have to work so hard." Maybe it's not fair, but that's the way it is.

Cheryl's persistence in making co-parenting work is one of the main things that makes it go well for us. She has really changed. She doesn't get angry at me much anymore, and when she does, she stops quickly and apologizes. I appreciate that, and it makes me want to reciprocate. Our whole relationship has changed, and I feel we work well together as co-parents. We both trust each other's intentions now. I don't feel she's trying to get me anymore.

I've been very fortunate to find myself in a loving relationship with a woman who also loves Sybil. I feel very lucky that she has been willing to put up with the hassle of dealing with a four-year-old child and has been so supportive of my co-parenting relationship with Cheryl, in spite of very natural feelings of jealousy. It is clear that she wants her relationship with me to work well, and, like Cheryl and me, she has put some of her uncomfortable feelings aside in order to make that happen. She and Cheryl get along well, and that has been a tremendous source of comfort and relief for me. It's made Sybil very happy, too. Last year, when Sybil had her birthday party and all of us went to it, she lit up, smiled, and said, "All my Mommies and Daddy are here today," and was able to share her affection with everybody. I think that Sybil is much richer because of her sense of being loved by so many different people.

One of the most important factors in making our co-parenting work well is Sybil herself. I think Sybil is a wonderful child, and she has adapted well to moving back and forth between homes. We let Sybil talk to Cheryl by telephone whenever she wants to, and she gets a great thrill out of dialing the number herself. I guess every parent is proud of his child, but somehow I'm not sure that all children would adapt to a co-parenting relationship as easily as Sybil has, and I have to give her credit for that.

Finally, I cannot underestimate the importance of good day care facilities in making co-parenting work for us. If we were unable to have Sybil taken care of during the day so that both of us could work at our separate professions, it would be extremely difficult for us to manage this situation. Sybil has gained a real sense of security and focus in her life from her school. It is the one place that she always returns to whether or not she is staying with Cheryl or with me. I also feel fortunate that the preschool she is going to is a very good one that meets both her intellectual and emotional needs.

By way of a summary, as I reflect on our first two years of co-parenting, the things that strike me most are not the intense, emotional feelings that Cheryl and I have had but the sense of resolve to make our commitment to Sybil work. I feel it is this overriding commitment to making co-parenting work for *everybody* which has allowed us to supercede our petty feelings.

Oliver Bjorksten, M.D., is Associate Professor of Psychiatry at the Medical University of South Carolina. Dr. Bjorksten went to the University of Wisconsin and the University of Wisconsin Medical School, and interned at Philadelphia General Hospital. He completed his psychiatry residency at the University of Pennsylvania, after which he became Director of Continuing Education at the Marriage Council of Philadelphia. Dr. Bjorksten specializes in marital and sexual therapy and is currently president-elect of the Society for Sex Therapy and Research. He also has supervisory status in the American Association of Marriage and Family Therapists. Dr. Bjorksten has four children, one of whom is being co-parented.

GERRY & DEREK
Long-Distance Co-Parenting

The impact of being a full-time co-parent hit me the day I tripped over Derek's sneakers. That was a little more than a year ago, Derek was then a 5'9" ninth grader who wore a size 10½ shoe.

We were sharing my two-room, Pullman-kitchen bachelor quarters. That's not the way I planned it, though. Karen, my former wife, and I had agreed that because of my new business, Derek would stay with her at least five days a week instead of our usual four day/three day co-parenting split. But when she had the opportunity to pursue a relationship in Colorado, she chose to do that—and Derek decided to stay in Philadelphia to be close to his Dad.

It was close all right. Derek slept on a hide-a-bed in a room that doubled as his bedroom and my living room. For six months, we struggled with the physical limitations of this space—dealing mostly with issues like whose dirty dishes were in the sink or why Derek's sweat socks weren't appropriate in the kitchen. I knew I had to get a larger place for us, at least for the next three years until Derek finished high school. Our move to our little two-bedroom row house was the start of a beautiful friendship.

During our mutual struggle just to find a place for ourselves, neither one of us (or at least I) hadn't realized that there was an adjustment process going on. Even though Derek could visit his mother as often as school holidays permitted, he wasn't going to have her there on a daily basis. In the beginning, it was obvious that he missed her and his older brother, who goes to college in Colorado.

This loneliness manifested itself in Derek's need to talk about his old family. Karen had left behind a big silver box filled with pictures and mementos. Derek often dragged this out of the basement, reliving his childhood as he sifted through the contents. (A fear he had when Karen and I first separated was that he would have to choose between us. "I thought if I chose my Dad, he'd feel great and my Mom would hate me, or if I chose my Mom she'd love me and my Dad would hate me," he wrote in a school paper.) I never discouraged Derek's lingering sense of family. I encouraged it, joining in and laughing with him at photos and stories both of us had heard many times before.

These moments, along with the fact that he now had his own room where he could be alone and surround himself with his personal belongings, created a safe environment for him. I made it clear, too, that this was his home and that even though it wasn't fancy, it needed both of us to take care of it. We started sharing responsibilities around the house—Derek washing dishes when I did the clothes or me the vacuuming the floor while he cleaned the bathroom. There was no system, but I feel, at this point, we began operating as a team.

There continue to be snags, however, particularly in our tastes for food and television. I have chosen to be more careful about what I eat and because of my hectic work schedule and other interests I don't watch television much except for an occasional ball game Derek and I watch together. I don't nag him about these things, though, but I have been very clear with him about how I feel. Somehow, I trust that my example and attitude have begun to present him with options.

Learning to trust Derek was a big but necessary step for me. When Karen was around, there was double-barrel control. We both kept after the boys. By myself, I perceived the situation as having only one barrel, which meant I had to trust Derek more. I realized this when I became concerned about his school work.

Derek is a bright kid, but he doesn't apply himself as much as I would like. He's crazy about athletics, but, as he and I know, it takes more than bouncing a ball to get into college. I felt his mediocre marks should be the issue of our first big talk. At that time, I placed the responsibility for his school work on him, assuring him that I was not going to peek over his shoulder every day to see how he was doing, or threaten to punish him. I just made it clear that getting what he wanted from life depended on him and that I would help when and where ever I could. But that talk didn't alleviate the guilt I continue to experience when I feel I should be available for him more often. When I'm not there as much as I think I should be, my anxiety level goes up.

In another talk, I approached Derek with these feelings of anxiety and learned that he likes a lot of independence. He's a teenager, and he doesn't want to be with his parents twenty-four hours a day. He admitted, in fact, to worrying about me being lonely when he's not around. We resolved this difference by promising to tell each other what we feel about being together.

On the other side of the coin, Karen is *very* available. She's conscientious about calling and writing Derek and since she's been away she's made the effort to come back to Philadelphia or fly Derek out to Colorado on an average of once every three months. Derek's reaction to this attention has proved to Karen and me that geographical and emotional distance are not necessarily synonymous.

Some people ask us, "But how can you have a joint custody arrangement when you live thousands of miles apart? These people think that time and proximity have to be a part of joint custody. But joint custody is not necessarily 3½ days on and 3½ off, time split evenly between mother and father, nor does it have to be determined by where each parent lives. It is an *attitude*—both mother and father participate in decisions related to parenting in an atmosphere characterized by openness, trust, and respect. Karen and I call one another frequently to discuss our sons. We each make a conscious effort to keep the other parent informed. Even though we are not geographically close, we consider ourselves close in the raising of our children. Neither Derek nor I doubt for one moment that his mother is available to him emotionally.

Being able to talk with my son about our relationship is a plus. Perhaps it stems from the feelings of closeness I have always had for him. I try to reinforce this bond with breakfast meetings at least twice a week. Over omelettes and French toast, we talk about anything. The other day, I asked him if he knew about sex and he said, "Oh, Dad," as he usually does when I ask something embarrassing. However, he admitted that he did have some questions. That has opened the door to other discussions. We talk about athletics, his latest batting average, and how important winning is to him. We talk about the draft and how frightened we both are of war. He tells me how messed up he perceives the world to be. I don't think there's anything he'd make a conscious effort to keep from me.

I think that Derek has matured through all of this ten times faster than he would have if he were still the youngest child in a family of four. We've both become co-supporters of the joint custody approach. He's appeared with me on television twice, once as a result of his testimony before a Senate subcommittee on legislation examining joint custody. He told that group, "I feel that because I am involved in joint custody, I have a better relationship with both my parents. I look forward to seeing them and because there is not as much tension in our household, I feel better about them and me."

During our years together, I see Derek and I becoming more like peers. We enjoy each other's company and are proud of each other. He even invited me to come to his school to speak before his religious thought class, and I take great delight in showing him off to my friends.

He's 6'1", in the 11th grade, and wears size 11 sneakers. But now I don't trip over them anymore.

Gerald B. Evans has masters' degrees in Divinity and Social Work. He is Founder and Director of the Men's Resource Center in Philadelphia, where he runs groups and workshops for men on issues related to separation, divorce, and other transitions. He is 5'5".

JENNIFER
Living With Two Sets of Rules

My co-parenting experience began in 1976. At the time, my two children, Robby and Kathy, were aged 13 and 12. The children's father and I had an arrangement (which had been in effect for several years) whereby I had the children during the week and he had them on weekends. In addition, he usually spent one or two evenings a week with them. Then, when he bought a house in my neighborhood, we decided to try co-parenting. The logistics were no problem: the kids could easily get to their neighborhood school from either house, they could socialize with their friends from either house, forgotten articles could quickly be retrieved, and they could move back and forth (every two weeks) with little effort.

However, I did worry about the fact that Bob and I were not on very good terms. Everything I had ever read or heard about co-parenting stressed the need for maturity and cooperation. I was not at all sure that it would work for us. Although we were basically civil, there was no love lost between us. Our value systems, lifestyles, and politics were not only different, they seriously clashed. This had a lot to do with why the marriage ended in the first place.

When it came to raising kids, things were no different. Bob was very traditional in his approach—children were a separate breed from adults. They were supposed to be well behaved, do well in school, know their place, and be a credit to their parents. My approach was different. As a political radical, I was committed to raising Rob and Kathy from a politically astute, antiracist, antisexist perspective. This meant that I taught my children always to question the way things were, never to respect authority blindly. I did this not so that they would agree with me, but so they would learn to think independently. I believed that the educational system was designed more to meet the needs of the state than to meet the needs of children. So I taught them that grades were important only in terms of survival and that getting good marks in school did not necessarily mean that you were intelligent, a creative thinker, or a good person. Although I believed that children should be well behaved, I also believed that they had rights, and that those rights should be respected, even by adults. I believed that racism could be as debilitating for whites as for blacks, so I pushed my kids to cross racial boundaries. I believed that sexism could be as devastating for males as for females, so I nurtured my son's gentleness and tenderness and built up my daughter's strength, self-confidence, and athletic ability. I believed that children are programmed and conditioned by society to believe in, support, and uphold the status quo, which is often unjust, so I provided my kids with alternative information regarding the system and how it operates.

Bob thought I was crazy. Never in his life had he heard of such a way to raise kids. He didn't understand it, and he didn't like it. And although he didn't overtly interfere with it, he did subtly try to undermine it. However, this did not change the co-parenting arrangement. Even though I didn't agree with or respect his approach, I *did* respect his right to equal time with his children.

So Bob and I more or less left each other alone in our dealings with Rob and Kathy. He dealt with them in his way, and I dealt with them in mine. Communication was minimal. Cooperation was even more minimal. Sometimes we would collaborate on unimportant things like buying Christmas gifts or coordinating vacations, but when it came to working on problems or issues together, or meeting the kids' emotional needs, we went our separate ways. It was a sort of live-and-let-live arrangement.

Incredibly, it seems to have worked out. Rob and Kathy learned to take the best from each of their disparate worlds. They learned to take in information, sort things out, and make their own decisions—about politics, lifestyles, and their own lives. They are both well-adjusted, creative, productive young adults.

Of course, they feel pulled back and forth from time to time, and they do feel that they did not have enough say in structuring the whole co-parenting arrangement. By and large, though, they are satisfied with how they are being raised—and so am I. I am glad that they had ample opportunity to experience both their parents, to benefit from what each had to offer. I am glad that Bob and I were able to go beyond our mutual dislike and mistrust and carry the whole thing off.

> *Jennifer Baker Fleming has co-authored two books on marriage and divorce:* Women in Transition *and* For Better, For Worse. *Her third book is* Stopping Wife Abuse: A Guide to the Emotional, Psychological and Legal Implications for the Abused Woman and Those Helping Her. *She hosts a daily radio show, "The Family in Transition," and is currently working on a book with the same title.*

KATHY
A Daughter's Viewpoint

Co-parenting started for me at the age of twelve. After my father bought a house in the same neighborhood as my Mom, we decided to spend an equal amount of time with him. We alternated houses every two weeks. I think my brother Robby and I accepted the idea pretty well and adjusted well.

It's kind of tough living with one person's values and ideas, then switching to a person who is the exact opposite. Sometimes I don't know what to think, but most of the time I try to combine the best ideas or values from both parents to create my own. It's worked out pretty well.

What I like about co-parenting is having two different homes, so just when you get sick of one parent, your time is up and you can get away from him or her. I think it would be very boring to live in one place with the same people for a long time, so I'm glad to have two homes.

I don't think co-parenting is bad, so I'm not embarrassed or ashamed to talk about it with any of my friends. In fact, I think that co-parenting has made me into a better, more balanced person by letting me experience two different lifestyles.

Kathy Fleming is the daughter of Jennifer Baker Fleming. She is sixteen.

BARBARA
A Step-Parent's View

I have felt different ways about co-parenting at different times. Relationships, even among families, are never static. What was true for us two years ago, or even two months ago, may not be applicable today. My husband Jeff had already worked out his co-parenting arrangement when I met him five years ago. Since I was a newly separated parent myself I was fascinated by his commitment to an intimate and ongoing relationship with his son. At that time, a man who made spending time with his young son a priority was rare. I was attracted to this quality in him, and it also suited my needs as a single parent. We could share parenting concerns. I was often around when Josh was with Jeff. Jeff was happy then, but it was hard when Josh left on Sunday mornings to be with Mimi. Jeff usually felt depressed for several hours following Josh's departure. This has changed completely over the years, and Josh's comings and goings fit nicely into our busy routine. Jeff and Mimi communicate freely, so if one parent feels the need to make contact with Josh or a problem arises they can see one another.

My son, Rick, and Josh share a loving relationship. Josh is two and a half years older than Rick, and they have had the opportunity to be together more than most children in step-parented families. Over the years, Josh has cared for Rick and watched out for his well being. This quality has endeared him to me, and I am glad that the boys share this. I think that they have the perfect amount of time to spend with one another. Unlike siblings, Josh and Rick have significant time periods away from one another. When they are reunited, their spirits are high and they have lots to talk about.

Becoming close and getting to know Mimi has been an unanticipated delight and reward. From the time I began to date Jeff, I saw they still liked one another. Fortunately, I was secure enough in my relationship with Jeff not to feel the need to

166

sabotage their bond. I felt then, as I do now, that for me to interfere would ultimately be a "losing situation" for everyone involved. After two years of avoiding one another, Mimi and I saw life would be simpler if we could find some way to relate.

I invited Mimi to go to a party with me. Jeff was out of town, and we used this as an excuse to get to know one another better. We had a wonderful time, and over the next few months we kept up our contact and began to include Jeff. I now consider Mimi one of my closest friends. She is a very special person who has always been available to me, shared her wonderful sense of humor, and has consistently been kind and generous to me. Recently our closeness and intimacy has confused us. The problem of describing the nature of our relationship has arisen numerous times over the course of five years. This particular summer, we have been questioning the meaning of the word "family" as it relates to us.

I frequently wonder what my role with Josh is. I spend less time with him than his mother does and yet more time than most women spend with their stepchildren. Jeff is a very concerned father and has always attended to Josh's needs—car pooling, visits to the doctor, school functions, playing, and buying clothes. Josh always turns to Jeff for help before turning to me. Mimi remains an active mother. She speaks frequently on the phone with Josh, buys birthday gifts, cooks, and shares her interest in music. Mimi arranges for music lessons and includes Josh in monthly musicals in her home.

What do I do? How am I special? What do Josh and I share? This has increasingly become a problem. Often, when we are left alone in one another's company, there are painful silences. These silences are somehow easier to bear when they occur with your own child. With Josh, I have sometimes felt, at these moments, that he was a stranger. This was poignantly brought home several months ago when Jeff was out of town for a few days. I assumed parental responsibility, but Josh was upset. He had difficulty falling asleep, tried to call his Mom, and left very early for school the next day in order to spend time at her house. I felt terrible. I had to ask myself why, when his mother lives two blocks away and he obviously wanted to be there, was I taking care of him? Co-parenting has been very successful in keeping both parents involved with Josh's daily life. However, at times, I feel superfluous to his life. If he came and spent a few days with us every other week, I might be able to overlook these problems. In fact, he is in our home on a regular basis, and I don't like the lack of connectedness that exists between us.

I have mixed emotions about the time Jeff and Mimi spend discussing Josh and his various needs. Sometimes, I am jealous. I miss the intimacy that occurs when parents discuss their child. I feel alone and left out. I resent their communication. A part of me is stirred up. Fortunately, I have learned to share these emotions. I also sometimes wonder what Josh really wants. I am certain that he wants to be with his parents, but now, after so many years of this arrangement, as Josh gets older his schedule may become a burden to him. If so, will he understand the situation, and will he be able to discuss the issues with his parents?

Mimi is a welcomed guest in our house. Jeff and I love to be with her. We speak daily. I have loved including her in my life. In turn, Mimi has brought traditional rituals which accompany Jewish family life back into my experience—all of us share a commitment to the family. Recently, however, tension has arisen around the question of where our commitments begin and end. We have tried to follow the traditional family ways. We have even tried to behave the way separated families live their lives. Yet as one of us deviates from these models, others feel jarred, left out, not considered, angry, and sad.

What is difficult for us to remember is that we are pioneers in this new form of family life. We need to create a form of parenting that suits everyone. For instance, this summer Jeff had to be away for six weeks. I knew that I did not want to carry on Jeff's part of the schedule. I looked forward to a break in the routine. I also longed to have a block of time, away from the group, alone with my son Rick. My decision raised a lot of questions. Jeff worried that Josh would feel rejected, and that Mimi would feel used and taken for granted. I resented their assumption that I would automatically maintain their schedule. After all, I had never been consulted about the parenting schedule.

I see that, to a certain extent, I maintain a distance. I wonder now if this distance allows me the option of choosing not to participate fully. I fight a sense of being swallowed in a maze of personalities, logistical arrangements, feelings, and parental duties. I see now that my decision to break the routine broke a certain homeostasis. I hope that what has emerged, although painful, will strengthen all of our relationships.

There are very special times when I do feel that Rick, Jeff, Josh, and I are a family. For several summers, the four of us have gone to a family camp in New Hampshire. I enjoy being among a group of people who know nothing about our situation. Here we present a picture of an all-American family. While I enjoy it, it also leaves me feeling confused.

One unsatisfactory area of my life is Mimi's relationship with my son, Rick. Most people would ask, "Why should Mimi have a special relationship with the other woman's son?" We are very close friends, supposedly part of a family. I treasure my friendship with her, as I know both Jeff and Josh do. I want Rick to experience her specialness. I am expected to give to her son. When Mimi comes to visit during the times Josh is with us we have dinner and talk. Usually all goes well. Josh knows that it is unacceptable for him to "act out" in our home. On the other hand, when Jeff, Rick, and I visit Mimi and Josh it is usually disastrous. I think that Josh feels invaded. He gets angry, wants Mimi's attention, and is annoyed with Rick. Mimi gets upset, but she protects Josh's feelings. Jeff feels helpless, and I get plain angry. We have talked about this pattern and are trying to avoid these pitfalls. I want Mimi to feel toward Rick as she might a nephew. Unfortunately, right now this is not the way it is. I feel disappointed and hope that things can change.

Sometimes I would like to move and leave all the schedules behind. Now that Jeff and I are married, I sometimes think of having a child of our own. Aside from obvious primitive pulls towards recreating our own family, I think these feelings stem from the part of me that wants separateness. Yet I recognize how special our arrangement is. I know that Jeff cherishes his time and involvement with Josh. There are areas in all our relationships that need work, refining, special attention. I do have the luxury of knowing we've worked out our ability to communicate. I know that problems can be worked on if the people involved are open and willing to try new ideas.

I am glad, that for myself, I do not co-parent. From the beginning, it was never an appropriate arrangement for me. I would not like Rick to leave each week or to be confined to the locale where his father lives. I enjoy the brief periods Rick visits his father; then I feel mobile. This arrangement suits me. Jeff, Mimi, and Josh have devised a way of life that seems to answer their particular needs. It has been both an honor and an adventure to be a part of their model. I look forward to the next chapter.

A Philadelphia artist specializing in color and whimsy, Barbara Julius became "related by marriage" to the author on April 6, 1980, when she married Jeffry Galper.

CAROLYN
Co-Parenting Within a New Life-style

Ian and I have been separated for four years. Our daughter, Jessie, is seven and in the second grade at a public Montessori school in Milwaukee. Jessie alternates weeks at each parent's house. Money is not an issue between Ian and me. We both pay Jessie's expenses when she is with us. We alternate claiming her as a tax deduction depending on whose taxes benefit that year, and we put the amount saved in her savings account.

I am as respectful of Ian as Jessie's other parent as he is of me. We are careful not to let tensions and squabbles get out of hand. Our schedule is rather structured, but we allow for flexibility. We have worked out holidays and vacations well; we manage with a little effort to keep toys and clothes at the appropriate home; in general, our co-parenting flows smoothly. Jessie is a lively, friendly, well-adjusted young girl, and her teachers and camp counselors, not blinded by parental pride, concur. Jessie understands the mechanics of the schedule (only once last year did she get on the wrong bus after school) and accepts in a matter-of-fact way that she has two homes. Jessie's concerns are typical for a seven-year-old girl: she wants long hair and is upset that hers isn't growing fast enough, she doesn't like to clean her room (but does like getting her allowance for it), she wishes she could have more slumber parties, she would enjoy going to McDonald's more often, and so on.

What has changed for me in the past three years are my feelings about being a parent. When Jessie was younger I was usually relieved—almost to the point of being joyous—when it was time for her to go to Ian. I found it overwhelming to work all day, manage our house, and be "on duty" for a toddler who seemed to demand my attention all the time—except when she was asleep. I felt that three and one half days per week of kid-energy were all I had (well, maybe three days). Fortunately, that was all I needed to summon. I didn't particularly like play-

171

ing children's games or reading bedtime stories. In fact, one night I finally responded to the nightly bedtime story request with, "Jessie, I just don't want to read your bedtime stories anymore except once in a while. Next time around, be sure to ask for a mother who's a bedtime story reader." Most of all I didn't like being interrupted all the time.

Now that Jessie is older things have changed. She is able to do most things for herself, which means I don't have to put so much physical energy into parenting. She is interested in doing many of the same things I am, which means we can play together in a way that is fun for me as well. We are always combing through the newspaper, for example, for movies we would both enjoy. I very much appreciate Jessie's curiosity about how the world works, and I like answering her questions and sharing my perspective on life. I want to see Jessie more than I do; I miss her a lot when she is away. I sometimes fantasize about what our life would be like if Ian dried up and blew away (this is in lieu of anything *bad* happening to him, of course). I won't try to change our present fifty-fifty schedule—I have just come to see more clearly the limitations of our situation.

I now also feel more a part of a family than I did three years ago, which makes it easier to be a parent to Jessie. At that time, I felt that Ian provided the better home. He lived with a woman, Sara, and her son Paul who is Jessie's age. I was always hearing about the fun, family-type activities they had. I imagined that Ian and Sara never uttered a single cross or harsh word. On the other hand, I was frazzled most of the time and hard-pressed to come up with mutually satisfying activities for Jessie and me. What I really wanted to do was spend my free time lying on the couch reading a book.

Three years ago, I fell in love with a woman named Kathleen, and a year later we moved in together. I am very pleased that I have found someone to share my life and parenting.

Things between Kathleen, Jessie and me did not go smoothly at first. As I look back (with the aid of some insights from a counselor we saw), we experienced the period of adjustment almost every blended family experiences. But at the time, it seemed we were hopelessly mixed up, our problems would never get resolved, and I would be forced to choose between my child and my partner. I felt I had to justify one's behavior to the other. And it upset me terribly when I heard them yelling at each other.

Our counselor was very helpful, and I recommend counseling, even short-term, for co-parents and step-parents who are having a rocky time. Our counselor pointed out that in some blended families certain members never like each other; to set up a goal that everyone be lovey-dovey is to invite disappointment. She suggested that I surrender my picture of the three of us as one happy family and let Kathleen and Jessie's relationship develop into whatever it was going to become. She also helped me see how much mediating I was doing and how that got in the way of Kathleen and Jessie working things out. So I have practiced keeping my mouth shut when the two of them get in a squabble. Kathleen and Jessie also spend some time together which doesn't include me, and this has helped them to appreciate each other.

Ian is supportive of Kathleen's and my relationship and of Jessie being with us, a plus not enjoyed by many lesbians. Ian is supportive because he knows that Jessie has a fun, loving home to be in when she is with me.

Over the last three years, my sense of being part of an extended family has increased. Sara co-parents with her ex-husband Tom, and through the children he has become connected to Kathleen and me. I remember the first time Tom called me. We had never spoken before, and he was calling to ask if his son Paul could spend the night with Jessie at my house. Tom and I have also cooperated on matters of mutual interest, such as pressuring Ian and Sara to install a second stairway to the third floor where the kids sleep so they can get out more easily in case of fire.

Initially, I had misgivings about Sara replacing me in Jessie's heart; those fears have passed. Sara is a warm, caring woman who is very loving with Jessie. She is also artistic, while I am not. She has taught Jessie about color, form, and texture. Sara is a patient teacher, while I am not. She has helped Jessie learn to read, swim and sew. Now if she would only get busy on teaching Jessie to ride her bicycle . . .

Last summer, Ian and Sara and Jessie and Paul spent two and one half months in a small town in Mexico, where Ian was enrolled in a language institute. I visited them for a week at the mid-point of their trip and appreciate how their family works, in particular Sara's role in it. But what finally put me over the edge into Sara's camp was the big family pow-wow Ian, Sara, Kathleen and I had last fall about changing our schedule, at Kathleen's and my request, from three and one half days at each house to a week at each house. After several hours of discusssion, it was clear to me that Sara, Kathleen, and I were much more on the same wavelength than Ian. I doubt that Sara and I will ever be close friends, but I am glad she is part of Ian's and Jessie's lives. I suspect that if she weren't, my dealings with Ian would be much more difficult.

Lest I paint too rosy a picture, let me make it clear that Ian and I do have our upsets. I become angry, for example, about the way he sometimes changes our schedule at the last minute or forgets about a schedule arrangement which I thought was already settled. Another difference is with their habits. Ian and Sara's house is disorganized. It's difficult to reinforce Jessie's tidiness and responsibility for her things, although it is not clear how much of this stems from the influence at Ian's house and how much is a typical seven-year-old's resistance. Ian, I suspect, has his own complaints about my style. I picture him muttering under his breath about how compulsive I am and how I am stifling Jessie's creativity. Considering all the possible struggles, I am pleased that Ian and I have an amicable relationship.

Our lives continue. Ian, Jessie, and I go out for dinner occasionally, and Jessie asks lots of questions about what Ian and I did with our lives before she was born. When my family visits Milwaukee for holidays, Ian usually drops by to say hello. Each parent and partner attends dance recitals and school potlucks. We take turns planning and hosting Jessie's birthday parties.

174

Periodically, we congratulate ourselves on how well we are doing, although we also notice that Jessie and Paul gravitate to school friends who come from very traditional families. What does this mean?

There is an important change coming up which will affect all of us. In two months, Kathleen will have a baby. Kathleen and I will provide the day-to-day nuturing. All of us, especially Jessie, are very excited about the coming addition to our family. Ian and Sara are pleased for us too, and have said they will make themselves available as part of our extended family for babysitting and other support. Check back with us in a few years for a progress report.

Carolyn Kott Washburne, M.S.W., is an Associate in Family Development at the School of Social Welfare, University of Wisconsin-Milwaukee, where she is on the staff of the Region V Child Abuse and Neglect Resource Center and teaches an undergraduate social work course on family violence. She was co-founder of the Women in Transition counseling program in Philadelphia and a founding board member of Sojourner Truth House, a shelter for battered women in Milwaukee. Of late, she has been exploring ways in which individuals and communities can achieve physical and emotional wellness.

CHUCK
The Clearness Committee

I am among the pre-jargon generation of co-parents. When I started out to share custody of my two daughters in 1974, there wasn't even a name for what my ex-wife and I were trying to do. Then the term "joint custody" was used almost as a term of obloquy. It may, in fact, be an exaggeration to call what we were doing then co-parenting, because we weren't so much co-parenting as simply declining to make use of the existing legal system against each other. In those days, Massachusetts' divorce laws were among the least progressive in the country.

In the meantime, we both moved to California, where the laws were more enlightened. Not terribly enlightened, mind you, but like night and day compared with Massachusetts. There you could do your own divorce, and we were advised that judges were inclined to accept custody agreements that were worked out in advance without much question. The do-your-own-divorce feature was a godsend. When I claimed pauper's status besides, the whole procedure ended up costing me about fifteen dollars. I couldn't have come up with much more at the time.

That left the sticky problem of negotiating a custody agreement. My ex-wife and I did not communicate too well (which, of course, had much to do with why we separated in the first place). But we both were lucky to be Quakers, and were in contact with the Quaker Meeting in Palo Alto, California, where we were both living in the spring of 1977. Quakers have an instrument called a Clearness Committee, which is used on various occasions, most often when a couple wants to get married "under the care of the Meeting." A Clearness Committee usually consists of three or four lay members, drawn from the Meeting in consultation with the couple involved; it meets with the couple, discusses as many relevant questions as the members can think of, and considers the responses until the members feel "clear" on a recommendation to the couple and/or the Meeting about the decision in question.

Obviously, this device appeared useful for a custody agreement, and the idea of a Clearness Committee for this purpose had occurred to us long before. But nobody we knew had actually been part of a Committee for settling custody, and that made me, for one, very nervous. In such circumstances I hate to be a pioneer; I much prefer to have others blaze the trail and make all the avoidable mistakes. But this time there was no way around it.

Our committee had four members. One was a psychologist, another an experienced early childhood educator—pretty good expertise to have for such an undertaking, not to mention the fact that they were all good people. We met four times, and after an initially tense opening session, got down to considering a draft agreement. Our meetings were several weeks apart; this was unavoidable because of the diverse schedules involved, but it is also a point of good Quaker practice—not to be hasty in weighty matters. We finished the agreement, which was accepted by all concerned, in July of 1977.

The Committee experience was clearly the turning point in our arrangement, because it got something on paper which we could live with and provided a model for revising it if the need arose. In fact, we haven't had to do that again, since we have thus far been able to negotiate changes in the terms informally. However, if the day comes when we can't do that, the agreement specifies that we must find another Clearness Committee to help us. And I think we will.

At this point, six years after we started, the co-parenting aspect of our relationship runs pretty smoothly. It has survived some pretty heavy challenges—two cross country moves, two marriages, alcoholism, poverty, and numerous local changes of residence, among others. Life seems somewhat quieter now for all concerned, but the future is, as always, an open question. Yet I have never doubted that co-parenting, difficult as it sometimes has been, was a far better alternative for me and my daughters than the traditional custody options. It has meant the difference between losing my parental status and maintaining it. That's not a small thing.

Chuck Fager is a writer who lives in Arlington, Virginia. He works for a Congressional committee as a staff writer. He has published three books, many articles and reviews, and recently became the father of a third daughter.

LYNNE
A Lawyer's Perspective

As a domestic relations lawyer, I help my clients sort out their lives, divide their property and get their divorces. Some people can reach agreement on the terms of their divorce with relatively little rancor. Many cannot. A not so small portion of my clientele become so consumed by the anger and vitriol of the process that it throws their lives into turmoil for years after the divorce decree has been handed down. One of the issues that inflames the passions of the disputants more than any other is the question of which parent will get the custody of the children. Too often, this is another chapter in the division of property.

The litigation of child custody creates a number of problems and offers few solutions. For the parents, it is expensive both in dollars (each parent may spend between $2,500 and $5,000 in legal fees); and in emotions (it is emotionally draining to spend so much time and worry trying to keep from losing their children). More important, it places the parents in such an adversarial position that they may never again be able to deal with each other effectively as parents.

For the children, the emotional trauma is enormous. Hives, stomach cramps, and vomiting are common symptoms in children whose parents are fighting over them. Not only are these children faced with the splitting up of their family for reasons they cannot understand, but they are then placed in the position of pawns in their parents' fight over custody. Frequently, they are forced to choose one parent over the other, a choice that often produces enormous guilt. Additionally, the children are frequently subjected to tremendous pressures and manipulations by either or both parents as they struggle for even the smallest advantage in their battle for the kids. And this is not a short process. Although trials concerning auto accidents or money damages will continue until completion, custody trials are often scheduled for a few hours one day and then perhaps four weeks later for another day. I've had custody trials that have spanned five or six months before the evidence is complete. This does not even take into consideration the appeal period, which may take up to eighteen months.

Nobody wins. The noncustodial parent, usually the father, is reduced to the status of favorite uncle, seeing the children for only brief periods at a time, having to become the mythical "super parent" to overcome all the daily interactions that no longer occur between parent and child. The child finds himself divorced from one of his parents, just as surely as his parents are divorced from each other. He cannot understand why. Once the court has awarded the child to one parent, that parent can manipulate the other by awarding or withholding additional time with the child in response to the other's behavior. The child is now a "thing" to be traded back and forth, and the courts are reluctant to hold the "naughty" parent in contempt for failure to comply with the court's visitation schedule. Now the time the child spends with the noncustodial parent becomes painful, and the relationship warps. As the children grow older, they begin to have plans of their own and frequently resent the rigid schedule they face in maintaining their relationship with their noncustodial parent. Even the custodial parent may find the taste of victory less than sweet. Instead of having help in making parental decisions, the parent stands alone. There are no days off, no substitutes, no one to fall back on in times of trouble. The adversarial process has done its work, and the parents can no longer consult each other over the childrens' problems. This is a heavy burden, and resentment is not an infrequent companion for the custodial parent.

Why do we handle child custody this way? The reasons are twofold and closely related. First, the legal precept of *stare decisis* must be understood. *Stare decisis* means that as matters were decided before so they will be decided now. In our glorious common law heritage, many legal rulings that are still valid were first handed down by judges of the King's Bench in England over 900 years ago. Laws set down when England was a feudal land, when wives and children were considered chattel (property)—before telephones, televisions, automobiles, walks on the moon—are still binding in our society today.

Fortunately, most legal concepts do not date back this far. In some legal areas, the courts are fashioning new principles where the old are found wanting. In other areas, the legislatures are reshaping and restructuring laws, shortcutting the legal reformulation process of the courts. Nonetheless, many antiquated laws still exist. One of the most odious is sole child custody. In the early part of the century and prior to that time, the father owned the children. Today, it is usually the mother. Once the marriage has ended, parenting has never been a joint proposition.

When parents fight over the children in the sole custody state, it is the court's obligation to weigh all the factors brought before it and then to determine which parent is the better. The court then places that parent in the position of being the sole judge of what is best for the child, allowed to determine how that child should be nurtured and brought up. The child is chattel, owned by one parent, and visited by the other parent like an animal in a zoo. The noncustodial parent is almost excluded from raising the child.

Certainly with the increasing awareness of fathers and their abilities as nurturing parents, mothers are no longer assured of receiving custody of their children in all cases. However, even in states that have an equal rights amendment to their constitution, such as Pennsylvania, mothers still end up with their children more than 90 percent of the time. Sole custody, however, is the decision in almost 100 percent of the cases. Rarely, if ever, do the courts assume that the children, who were born to two parents, should continue to have the love of both, even after divorce and separation. The child loses. Not only do the parents split, but the children are given to one parent only.

We have failed to realize that while parents may not be able or desirous of dealing with each other as husband and wife, they can still usually cooperate as parents. We find it necessary to intercede in the parent/child relationship when a marriage fails, but not when it succeeds. (The courts don't recognize that there is no correlation between success as a spouse and success as a parent.) Even if both are good parents, we find it necessary to evaluate and to choose between them. That is Solomon's choice. The fact that parents cannot get along with each other is no reason to deprive a child of one of them.

It does not have to be that way. A simple solution called joint custody lies close at hand. Let the parents share the joys and the pains of raising the children they brought into the world. Let the courts presume what nature presumes—a child born with two parents keeps two parents, despite a divorce. Several states, like California, have legislated joint custody into their family law systems.

Joint custody maintains the family much more closely than sole custody ever did. The nuclear family survives between child and parent if not between husband and wife. An expensive and unnecessary court fight between parents is avoided. It helps to promote happy, healthy children with two parents.

The arguments against joint custody are many, if not convincing. First, if two people cannot get along together in a marriage, how can they expect to function together as parents in making the decisions that will shape their child's life? Second, the child of divorced parents needs the stability of one home, one set of friends, one set of rules. Third, the child will be confused about where he lives. Finally, sole custody is how things have been done in the past, so that is how they should be done in the present (our old friend *stare decisis*).

In reply, I point out that people often stay married for many years, even hating each other intensely, because they do not want to hurt the children. That kind of self-sacrifice is exactly the same personal quality that will enable parents to deal with each other as parents, even when they cannot do so as husband and wife.

I have a number of clients who have joint custody—some have worked it out between themselves, while others have had it imposed by a wise judiciary. I remember three cases involving parents who hate each other. The six children involved range in age from 7 to 15 years. All three situations involve month-long custody with each parent. In one case, both parents live in the same school district. (The judge refused to sign the joint custody order as he didn't believe in the concept, but the parents chose to operate, in the best interests of their children, away from the courts.) In a second case, the parents live in two counties, Chester and Philadelphia, but the child is in a private school. The third case involves a two-county set of parents in which the father drives the children to school in the mother's county when he has custody. None of these parents talk to each other; but they also don't denigrate the other parent to the children. And the children are thriving!

Children need parental stability, the love and guidance of both parents, more than superficial stability such as housing accomodations and school friends. The bedrock of any society is its families. Even when parents divorce, children can retain a strong, working relationship with both and never lose a parent to divorce. And the children always know where they live. They would rather remember a schedule than lose a parent.

Joint custody is a developing concept whose time is drawing near. It is pro-family. It is a radical change for the judiciary and will educate parents to the concept that children are not tools to manipulate.

Lynne Gold-Bikin is a lawyer specializing in family law. She is a Lecturer in Law at Temple Law School, Temple University, Philadelphia, Pennsylvania, as well as a Lecturer in Law with The Pennsylvania Bar Institute's Continuing Legal Education Institute for the lawyers of Pennsylvania. She has coauthored a Law Review article on the Pennsylvania divorce code and has contributed to the drafting of the new divorce code.

MIRIAM
An Update on the Law

Within the past year, I was asked to testify as an expert witness in the case of a father who wanted joint custody, an ex-wife who was adamantly opposed to it, and two children, ages 9 and 11, who wanted to live with both parents. I knew the parents because they had been in counseling with me. The father had read the first edition of this book and wanted to reverse the legal agreements that had been drawn up when the separation first took place some years ago. He wanted joint custody, instead of his ex-wife having sole custody. He wanted the time and luxury of being more involved with his children, to see them more, to be actively involved in their lives—not just on vacations. He wanted a say in where they went to school, and he wanted to reconsider the financial agreement he had signed. Mostly, he wanted to be with his kids as part of their daily routine. The mother, on the other hand, didn't want her life to change. She like things just the way they were, I felt for her. Here she was, a woman whose life was defined by her home, her children, her new husband and his family. She had had sole custody of her children for several years following the separation and divorce, and now she was being asked to give up what she considered to be her main function in life. If the children would be with their father for long periods of time, what would she do with herself? It was no small thing, and it is something that terrifies many women when they contemplate joint custody. You really have to face who you are, what your identity is, what is life about if the children aren't always with you. And this was a woman with interests, social relationships, and an active life.

During the course of counseling, they were unable to come to any agreement, any compromise, any position that would get them out of a custody battle in the court. It was a tense scene—a parent on each side of the aisle, with their staunch supports, family and friends who had lined up on one side or the other. It was sad too, that it had come to this. It had cost each parent a lot of money. And both parents felt morally right in upholding their position.

My testimony was about the importance of *both* parents having an intimate relationship with their children, one that was ongoing in the daily comings and goings of life, one that was not relegated to vacations. I said that I thought both parents were fit, upright, stable members of their community, were equally loving and capable of taking care of their children. The judge asked me many questions. He was especially concerned with the best interests of the children and was afraid that moving back and forth between two homes would create problems for them. I said that I thought more problems would be created if they were not as close to their father as they wanted to be.

One interesting thing came up. The lawyer for the defense, the mother's lawyer, pointed out that in this book I had clearly stated the need for trust, respect, cooperation, and communication between two parents in order for joint custody to be effective. My answer was that I had changed my mind. I no longer thought that an important relationship—that of a father (usually) to his children—could be put aside just because the mother was unwilling to cooperate. She could be ordered to cooperate by the court (although you can't legislate good will), and that this step was worth taking because of the relationship the children could have with the father. I say father here, because he is usually the parent who has to fight for a close relationship with his kids, but really I mean all noncustodial parents.

The judge decreed, in a precedent-setting case in Pennsylvania, that there be joint custody. The children would be with their father for five straight months, seeing their mother on weekends. The summer vacation would be evenly divided, and then five months would be spent with the mother, with their father seeing the children on weekends.

I ran into the father on the street the other day, and he told me that everything is working out well. The children are dropped off and delivered as they should be, the arrangements have worked out smoothly. He has no regrets at all about pressing the issue to the fullest extent possible.

Testifying in this case made a lasting impression on me. I was glad to have had the opportunity to speak of a position that I feel strongly about, and I was glad to be able to make a contribution to the laws in this state. But the whole process seemed degrading to all the participants, and it didn't feel like a victory to me to have the father win his case for joint custody.

Recently, I was asked to testify at hearings of the Senate Judiciary Committee of the State of Pennsylvania on the same subject. Two new bills were being considered, to complement Pennsylvania's new divorce laws. One states that both parents have to agree to joint custody. The other states that even if only one parent wants joint custody, it must be considered by the court. What interested me was that, much like the new legislation in California, both bills provide that if one parent is granted custody, it should be granted not on the basis of sex but on the basis of which parent is more likely to allow frequent contact with the noncustodial parent. If a parent is fighting for sole custody, wanting to prove the other parent unfit, that parent is now less likely to get sole custody. The assumption is that a parent who is so adamant about sole custody would not be as willing to allow the child to have a positive relationship with the other parent. It's a crucial point. The goal of this kind of legislation is to protect the child's need to have an open, easy relationship with both parents.

The hearing was held in a bare courtroom in City Hall, in downtown Philadelphia. How could anything civil take place here? Did the state senators really want to know what I thought? Were they really interested in my testimony? There were a lot of people scheduled to speak that day—a judge opposed to joint custody, the president of Father's and Children's Equality, two children who had gone through two custody trials, lawyers, a social worker who directs the Men's Resource Center in Philadelphia. What I saw immediately, much to my amazement, was that these legislators really *did* care about having more humane legislation in Pennsylvania, and they were deeply concerned about what would be in the best interests of the children as well as the parents. I was moved by the legislative process that was taking place. I felt humble.

Here is a portion of my testimony:

People often ask just how two people who are divorcing can possibly be civil enough toward one another to work out joint-custody arrangements. My answer to that is that there is a prevailing myth that once you are divorced, you no longer have to deal with your ex-spouse. Whatever the custody arrangements, there will always be dealings between parents, whether they are financial, or whether they concern what school the child should go to, how to handle special events, and so on. Certainly, life is easier all around when you can put your bitterness and anger aside and work out your dealings with your ex-spouse. If that is not the case, the children should not be denied the right to an intimate, caring relationship with both parents. Children should not be the victims of their parents' immaturity or their continuing anger toward one another. Children have a right to a close relationship with both parents, whether those parents like it or not, and whether those parents trust and respect each other or not. This view is different from that which I expressed in my book three years ago.

I know many people who have divorced, can't stand each other, and manage to work out joint custody. What they have learned is that it is in their children's best interests for them to get out of the way and allow their children to be close to the other parent. If they can't talk to each other enough to work that out, they can use friends, relatives, or lawyers. Interaction can be minimal and on a specific schedule. A child's relationship is too important—precious really—to be dictated by whether or not those parents can maintain a civil relationship with one another.

Another criticism of joint custody is that it is just too confusing for the child. I think that it is more confusing for the child to wonder where his father went, why he doesn't see him too often anymore, and to feel that perhaps he is not loved. That is confusing. Children are confused by separation and divorce. There is no question that it is an upheaval in their lives. But the research is showing that it is of vital importance to the emotional well-being of the child to maintain close ties with the parent who leaves home—usually the father. Children are quite flexible and at a young age are able to learn what their schedules are. The continuity and stability in their lives comes from the love they receive from both parents, and from the knowledge that their parents, even though no longer married, are willing to go to great lengths to be with them on an ongoing basis.

The children who testified at the Senate hearing (they were 14 and 12) said that their father wanted joint custody and they wanted joint custody, but that after each court battle they were returned to live with their mother full-time. Another young boy testified that when his parents first separated, he was terrified that he would have to choose one parent over the other, and whichever parent he chose, the other would be mad at him and not love him anymore. He was very relieved when his parents told him he'd be living with both of them.

There have been some changes, some new legislation. California, Oregon, Iowa and Wisconsin have adopted joint custody legislation. Although it is permissible for parents to ask for joint custody in other states, these states are the only ones that specifically provide for this option.

There has also been some attention from the media. The February 4, 1980, issue of *Time* stated that "More and more, single Dads are rearing their children. While women still get custody in the overwhelming majority of divorces, between 1970 and 1978 the number of children over 18 living with divorced fathers jumped by 136 percent; close to 500,000 divorced American fathers are now rearing sons and daughters without the help of a wife, At the same time, many other ex-spouses are trying another fast-spreading arrangement, joint custody, in which father and mother share the responsibilities for the rearing of their kids."

It is still controversial, however, and that is what troubles me. It seems to me to be the most natural thing in the world—two parents bring a child into the world and they have the responsibility of taking care of that child. Perhaps that is too simplistic. In any case, there has been some movement in the legal arena since this book was written and more and more states are beginning to update their laws to reflect the changes taking place in society.

It *is* possible to change the statutes, and it is up to people who are concerned about these issues to pressure their state legislators to make the necessary changes. I recently heard of one judge in Philadelphia who would not sign an order for joint custody, even though *both parents* wanted it. He said he didn't believe in joint custody. What is he doing on the bench? That gets up the *irate citizen* in me.

A biographical sketch of Miriam Galper appears on page 207 of this book.

JAY
An Alternative to Co-Parenting

My first wife and I were divorced eight years ago. We had three sons: Jay, Jr., age 18; George, age 15; and Andy, age 12. The divorce was particularly vicious. At the time, I had a successful small business, and I had also met the woman I wanted to make my second wife, Ann. Ann had two children herself: Mia, age 9, and Becky, age 7. Ann believed that it was possible for us to create a kind of extended family situation in which my sons and her daughters would be an integral part of our new lives. Indeed, she always assumed that we would have my children with us for continuous periods of time and that while we would never try to preempt my sons' natural affection for their first mother, Janet, we could provide them with another home, a second family that would have its own importance in their and our lives.

In the course of three years of litigation, with legal fees of over seventy thousand dollars, she and I learned differently. In the eyes of the court, Ann was "the other woman," my "paid paramour." While she was raising two of her own children quite successfully, she was an adulteress, a de facto unfit mother. The litigation demanded our constant and unremitting attention because the contending parties had to show that their respective spouse was really the cause of all of the ensuing difficulties and that the other partner was really quite blameless.

There is a sharp disjunction between the psychological dimension of a couple's relationship and the adversary position the law in many states still forces couples to take. I reached the apex of this juridical posturing when our respective lawyers suggested that we persuade our children to take the stand in court and testify against their father or mother. One can easily imagine the psychic damage done to a youngster at any age when he or she is asked to repudiate a parent in a public court of law. In the long run, what could be more unnatural or bar-

baric? How is the child supposed to choose? On what basis? It is like asking a child which arm he would like to lose, the left or the right? Such a choice is no choice at all, and while my first wife had made preparations to go ahead on this basis, I could not because I felt then, and believe now, that there is no "victory" under such conditions.

Meanwhile, constant psychological stress—the drained emotions, and the perpetual care required to file yet another brief and yet one more rejoinder to the other side—was distracting Ann and me from attending to pressing matters in our company; before long, there were no more contracts "in the works," no more business to be done. Frankly, I lacked the energy and drive to bring in the new projects upon which the company's existence was predicated. The result of this was that I had to dissolve the company, and while I never had to claim bankruptcy, some creditors had to wait several years before they were fully paid. The entity that had taken ten years to build was snuffed out, along with the livelihoods for both families.

The person who took it the hardest was my youngest son, Andy, who was least able to cope with the extraordinary emotional traumas generated by the divorce. He understood the least of what was going on. Perhaps the most sensitive, he was the most caught up by Janet's incandescent rage. She was often out of control. She could afford to be "crazy" because in the eyes of the law she was the wronged mother of three sons, the injured party, the exploited spouse who was entitled to everything she could get—and more.

One evening, she sat my sons down and proceeded once again to tell them what a terrible person their father was and how seditious and deceitful Ann was. As her diatribe reached its fevered pitch, Andy snuck off into his room, opened the window, and began to lift himself over the guard rail so that he could smash his body on the concrete sidewalk five stories down. Jay, Jr., heard the sound of the window being opened and rushed into the room in time to drag him back from the sill to the floor. A few hours later, I was told that Andy had been commited to Bellevue Hospital for psychiatric observation because of an attempted suicide.

I cannot describe the anguish and guilt that I felt for Andy's plight as I visited him in the ward over the next few weeks. We sat and talked day in and day out, and I had the sense that I was talking with an amnesiac who had successfully murdered his own past so that he would feel no more painful memories. My son, George, held me responsible for everything that had gone wrong—as he saw it, I had taken up with Ann and abandoned them all—and asserted that he never wanted to see me again. Eight years later, I can attest to the fact that George has been as good as his word, and we have never seen one another over those years, in spite of calls and letters on my part.

With Andy in the hospital, my business in dissolution, and Janet on a renewed and revitalized attack, Ann surrendered and retreated to her bed. For days and then weeks, she stayed in that bed with the covers over her head, refusing to come out. Of all the parties, she had been the strongest. It was she who had brought the Christmas presents to the boys at the lawyer's office—I was not allowed in the house to visit them. It was she who made sure all of the birthdays were remembered. It was she who recounted the particulars of all the various incidents Janet's lawyer used against us so that my lawyer could file the required rejoinders. It was Ann who had been "the inside man" in the company to see that projects were completed on time and within their projected costs. It was she who was my business partner, my friend and supporter, and my hope for a new life. It was she whom I loved (although that love was mired in guilt and rage and often despair). When Ann could go on no more, I knew that we would have to find some other way out.

The lawyers finally settled out of court because I instructed my lawyer to agree to whatever demands were made by the other side. He did his best, but in truth he had always been fighting a rearguard action—partly because I had never given him the "ammunition" he needed to fight with and partly because I had made no secret of the fact that I was living with Ann. Under these conditions, there was very little he could do.

Appendix

The resulting settlement called for my turning over all of my assets to Janet: the three parcels of land, the car, the savings account. In other words, all material goods. The combination of alimony, child support, tax payments, and other sundries amounted to between two thousand and three thousand dollars per month. Even if my company had continued, I knew that I could never pay that much and have any money left over for living expenses. The assets of over one hundred thousand dollars that had been built up over the years were gone (with Janet's lawyer taking the lion's share so that my family was never to reap any of their possible benefits), the business had a few months left in it, and the obligations represented by the settlement terms to begin within a month.

Andy's psychiatrists recommended intensive individual and group therapy, a specialized school setting because of his emotional disturbances, and various other types of support services which were now beyond my means. Ann and I had stopped paying the rent on our apartment, and the landlord was threatening eviction. We had gone on unemployment insurance because the company could no longer afford to pay us. Since Janet had to transfer the assets she had obtained from me to her lawyer in payment of the legal fee, all of the parties were without money. My lawyer had been my friend and so had agreed to defer payment of his thirty-five-thousand-dollar fee. (Many years later, this fee was finally paid.)

Thus we were without money or an income sufficient to live in New York City. We were also in need of human services. Ann's daughters, Mia and Becky, had been kept out of most, but certainly not all, of the vicious charges and countercharges. (The girls added the new vocabulary word "paramour" to their verbal repetoire early in life.) When Ann had the opportunity to leave New York and visit a friend in the Caribbean, the girls and I urged her to go. Under pressure from us, she finally assented. Several weeks later, Ann called to say that she did not want to return to New York, but wanted the three of us to follow her down there. The girls and I quickly agreed, and we proceeded to collect and sell the final asset that we had: the antique furniture that Ann had collected over the years. With the three thousand dollars we got from the sale, we were able to buy our plane tickets and leave the apartment before the landlord repossessed it for nonpayment of rent.

Ann also had one other suggestion: kidnap Andy and bring him with us. She felt that Janet's behavior amply justified this action. She further believed that Andy would be effectively destroyed as a person if he were to remain with his natural mother. (Subsequent events bore this out.) Janet had done everything in her power to destroy my credibility as a father in Andy's eyes. Had I not been unfaithful to his mother? Had I not left the family? Had I not stopped supporting them? For one parent to destroy the credibility of the other parent is unconscionable because a youngster's sense of his own identity demands that he internalize both role models. For this reason, I had always been careful never to criticize Janet in front of the boys. I knew that no matter what I might think of her, my sons needed her for their own consequent psychological survival.

I did not kidnap Andy and neither did I see him for several years. Janet would not allow him to visit us in the Caribbean because Ann was an "evil, reprobate adulteress" who would scheme to win the affection of our son and woo him away from his natural mother. There was really little I could do about this since I had no rights under the settlement and for all practical purposes had been negated as a father but not as an economic provider. I fulfilled neither function, and my only contact with my sons was with Jay, Jr., who did come to the Caribbean against his mother's wishes, and did stay with us. This association with Jay meant a great deal to all of us, including Becky and Mia, who had always felt they had older brothers who someday would be part of the family.

When Ann and I finally married, Jay, Jr., was my best man. That was a great moment for me, but his association with our family was often very difficult for him. If he relaxed and felt happy with us, he believed that he was betraying his mother and perhaps even his brothers. Jay felt guilt about his own happiness. He knew that whether he spent an evening or a month with us, he would be cross-examined when he returned home to Janet. To this day, Jay has not surmounted many of the inchoate and confused feelings he has in his relationship to us, even though of all of my sons he has been the most loyal and ultimately the most knowledgeable about what happened. But even Jay has not really been able to put it all together in a way that makes his life work better for him.

True, he is finishing college now, after several false starts, and rightfully feels quite proud. But he still lacks a certain kind of emotional perspective, an integration of his past, that will properly empower him to manage his own emotional relationships with women, and ultimately with other human beings. Jay, Jr., is deeply scarred but he does continue to grow, and he is still young enough to heal.

George has not seen me in eight years, and the last time I talked to him on the phone, he yelled an obscenity at me and commanded that I never call the house again. Shortly after this incident, the phone number was changed and once again unlisted. In many ways, George is an amazement to his brothers, as he is to me. He drives around with a shotgun in the back of his car. He is, his brothers tell me, "a redneck" who likes to get into fights and "kick ass." He has managed to become his father's antithesis—as I was part of the civil rights movement in the sixties and seventies, so George wants "to shoot the niggers." Disturbed, exploitative in his relationship with others, prejudiced, unwilling to talk about his feelings or to attempt any relationship with me, George will probably spend his emotionally confused life in a morass of unrequited anger and unceasing and unresolved rage. Without resolution of such overpowering emotions, what hope can there be for this youngster who at one time in his life liked to fish and farm, lift weights, and play basketball?

About a year ago, Andy finally came to stay with us, at his mother's suggestion. It seems there had been some "trouble" and Andy had narrowly avoided being either killed or imprisoned. Over the years, Andy had been allowed to use drugs at home and to engage in petty robberies in the neighborhood.

At one point, he was held overnight in jail but no charges were brought because there was insufficient evidence against him. These events were the culmination of years of being allowed to do just about anything he wanted to, dropping out of school, and taking up with criminals.

Andy stayed with us for over six months until things quieted down and then, much against our wishes, as well as those of Jay, Jr., he returned to Janet's neighborhood, where he obtained a job as a messenger. While he still manages to avoid open conflict with the law, he is still mired in actions for which he may face possible death or imprisonment. He remembers little of his past life—the camp experiences and friends he made, his teachers, the time all of us spent together as a family sledding in the Vermont snow and swimming in brooks, the books we read together. For Andy, none of this ever happened, and it is easy to understand why. Andy's life is now defined in terms of the street, the successful robberies, his present friends, his monotonous job—and the big heist to come before he turns twenty-one. He was the gentlest of us all, the most accepting, the kindest, and now potentially the most violently aggressive.

Mia is in college, and Becky in high school. They are the best integrated of all the children, primarily because, in spite of the vicissitudes of their lives, they have always been loved and cared for. Of the children, they are the luckiest and, along with Jay, Jr., have the most promise of leading a full and loving life. (Their natural father deserted them when they were still preschoolers. He has never contacted them or their mother. Shortly after Ann and I married, I legally adopted them.)

Ann and I have survived, and our relationship is still strong, but in different ways we have both suffered and paid the existial price of our union. Whatever dreams we shared of an extended family have been conclusively shattered. The crucible of many of these last years has deepened our feelings for one another, but we have been through a great deal and there has been little sustained joy. We have never been able to share my sons or to construct another vehicle like our company to exploit our talents and contribute to the larger society. Janet works giving private music lessons. There is little joy in her household, and, according to two of our sons, "little love."

This is just one man's story, but it is, of course, much more than that. It is actually the story of eight people, all of whom, I feel, have suffered more than they should. While adults must take responsibility for their own actions, the social framework within which this human drama was enacted is also part of the story. It is only within the last few years that the concept of shared custody or co-parenting has developed. At the time of my divorce, it was understood that children were always best off with their mother. It was understood that the male's function was basically economic. No-fault divorce simply did not exist. As I see it in retrospect, the only people who made out were the lawyers. Their legal fees absorbed all of the assets. The legal system postulated an adversary framework fought out by hired guns, prepared to litigate if their fees were insured. Such a framework has little to do with the emotional and material needs of everyone but the lawyers. Surely I must take my share of the blame, but my wife was never blameless or guiltless either. The issue should not have been to apportion guilt or mete out punishment.

The central strength of co-parenting is that the focus is shifted from the games of the parents to the needs of the children. Our children should not have been forced to pay the emotional price they did. In different ways and to varying degrees, they have all been affected by the divorce. The central issue should have been the welfare of the five of them and how the respective parties were to responsibly contribute to that welfare, both emotionally and financially. The present social order—and make no mistake about this—is latently violent. Otherwise, how else could an adult, any adult, seriously suggest that a child testify against any parent in a court of law? Why else would a lawyer ask for damaging acts commited by the spouse, whether or not such acts ever occurred? Was it appropriate that ten years of sweat and hard work be tossed down the drain because I found another person with whom I wanted to spend my life? Was it just that Andy could be driven to self-destruction? Was it fair that I was denied access to my children? Was it right that Mia and Becky hear at the ripe old age of nine and seven that their mother was a "paramour"?

Co-parenting begins with the premise that it is in the best interests of the child to have both parents on some agreed-upon basis. Both parents contribute their lives, their money, their energy to the offspring they have voluntarily decided to have. Had such a spirit been part of my divorce, then I believe that the story recounted in these pages could have been quite different. Not perfect, mind you, but not the still unresolved emotional morass that even now afflicts us. The alternative to co-parenting is some variant of the tale I have just told. What is so frustrating is that if we had had a framework through which our emotional drives were channeled into productive environments for our children, the ego tripping of any one party would have been prevented with respect to the detriment of the other.

Whether my personal account is biased or not is in this sense totally unimportant. The system—that is, the social and legal system—should be biased in favor of the children, and co-parenting requires that the adults turn away from their anger, their blasted hopes, their frustration over failure, their childish impulses to destroy, their self-pity, their melancholia, their loneliness, and their despair—in short, the whole apparatus of their damaged egos and pride—and to reconstruct the world of their children so that they have some chance of growing up whole people.

This is the great strength of co-parenting and it is also its fundamental weakness because there will always be those who cannot grow up to the responsibility of adulthood. They are simply not able to put away the things of children and to assume their accountability as parents. The choice is up to each of us.

Jay Wald, a pseudonym, presently works in the field of international education. He is the author of several books and articles on education and the schools. He has chosen to write under a pseudonym to protect his children.

Selected Readings

The Boys and Girls Book About Divorce, by Richard A. Gardner, M.D. New York: Bantam Books, 1971. $1.25, 157pp. A good book for children, written clearly and with sensitivity.

The Parents' Book About Divorce, by Richard A. Gardner, M.D. New York: Bantam Books, 1977. $2.95, 220pp. I don't know why, but I am amazed that Dr. Gardner speaks highly of joint custody. He is an authority in the field of divorce and his word means a lot. It's also a practical, helpful book.

Surviving the Break-up: How Children and Parents Cope with Divorce, by Judith S. Wallerstein and Joan Berlin Kelly, New York: Basic Books, 1980. $18.50. This big book is the result of a five-year post-divorce study of sixty families in California. It's a major piece of work in the field because it provides clinical evidence, based on research, to show that a child's relationship with his or her father is crucial to the development of the child's mental health after divorce. The authors found that the adjustment of the child depends more on what happens *after* the divorce than in the predivorce family. It's well written, interesting, and probably not worth the price. It's bound to be out in paper soon.

Divided Children: A Legal Guide for Divorcing Parents, by Michael Wheeler. New York: W.W. Norton, 1980. $10.95, 224pp. This book deals primarily with the legal aspects of custody. There is a fine chapter called "The Best of Both Parents" in which Wheeler details the negative judicial attitude about joint custody. He explains that this attitude is unsubstantiated, and that it is based on sheer bias on the part of lawyers and judges. An important differentiation is made between legal and physical custody.

Children of Divorce, by J. Louis Despert, M.D. New York: Doubleday, 1962. $2.50, 298pp. Originally published in 1953, this book is a classic. Dr. Despert was one of the first professionals to speak of divorce as not necessarily traumatic and destructive for children. She feels that it is "the emotional situation in the home, with or without divorce, that is the determining factor in a child's adjustment."

The Courage to Divorce, by Susan Gettleman and Janet Markowitz. New York: Ballantine Books, 1975. $1.75, 267pp. An excellent book which challenges assumptions about divorce made by mental health professionals, the courts, and the media. Highly recommended.

Creative Divorce: A New Opportunity for Personal Growth, by Mel Krantzler. New York: New American Library, 1975. $1.95, 268pp. This is a very popular book, a bit slick and not one of my favorites. One chapter I did like was about children, "Seeing the Person in the Child."

How To Get It Together When Your Parents Are Coming Apart, by Arlene Richards and Irene Willis. New York: Bantam Books, 1977. $1.75, 171pp. This book is geared towards teenagers and is especially strong in the section dealing with questions of custody. The authors encourage teenagers to voice their preferences concerning which parent they want to live with, and to ask to see the part of their parents' separation agreement that deal with custody, child support, and visitation rights. I like that idea very much.

MOMMA: The Sourcebook for Single Mothers, edited by Karol Hope and Nancy Young. New York: New American Library, 1976. $3.95, 388pp. MOMMA began as an organization of single mothers and now includes single fathers as well. The organization publishes a newspaper, and this book is a collection of some of the articles which appeared there, as well as new material. MOMMA contains personal accounts of women and men who are single parents, and a lot of hard, factual material. The section on co-parenting is well worth reading.

Part-Time Father, by Edith Atkin and Estelle Rubin. New York: Signet Books, 1977. $1.75, 181pp. An excellent book for fathers who have visitation rights. The authors are opposed to what they call shared custody, and there is a small section on fathers who have full custody of their children.

The Custody Handbook, by Persia Woolley. New York: Summit Books, 1979. $10.95, 350pp. I like this book a lot. It's a comprehensive survey of all child-custody arrangements. Ms. Woolley clearly prefers what she calls "shared custody." She tells why and delineates the steps parents and children need to take in order for it to work out.

The Disposable Parent: The Case for Joint Custody, by Mel Roman and William Haddad. New York: Holt, Rinehart and Winston, 1978. $8.95, 215pp. This book is geared to parents as well as to professionals in the legal and counseling fields and speaks to the need for changes in the legal system to support joint-custody arrangements. This is an important book and I recommend reading it.

Women in Transition: A Feminist Handbook on Separation and Divorce, by Women in Transition, Inc. New York: Charles Scribner's Sons, 1975. $6.95, 538pp. I am biased when it comes to reviewing this book, since I was part of the collective which wrote it. It really is a good book, a very comprehensive (if a bit long-winded) guide covering emotional supports, children in transition, what the law says, the economic realities of separation and divorce, education resources, mental health, physical health care, and consumer protection information. There is some information regarding shared custody, but not a lot. It's a large-format paperback and worth the price.

Making it as a Stepparent: New Roles/New Rules, by Claire Berman. New York: Doubleday and Co., 1980. $8.95, 202pp. A down-to-earth, practical book dealing with such topics as "The Blended, Merged, Combination, His and Hers Stepfamily," "S-E-X," "The Visitors or Weekend Family." It's easy to read and good too.

What Every Man Should Know About Divorce, by Robert Cassidy. Washington, D.C.: New Republic Books, 1977. $8.95 cloth, 246pp. This is a well-written book which offers a lot of practical advice and emotional support for the divorced man. There is one page devoted to joint custody, and it is a good one. I like this book, and I think it is a needed addition to the available literature on divorce.

Single Father's Handbook, by Richard H. Gatley, Ph.D. New York: Anchor Books, 1979. $4.95, 196pp. The assumption in this book is that fathers are separated from their children as well as from their wives. It is a helpful guide on how to be with your children on a part-time basis. They suggest, "Be a good co-parent. Be the best partner you can." I like that.

Acknowledgments

Support comes in many forms. A friend will call at 2 A.M.
because she knows I am writing and wants to say she is thinking
of me. Someone else will ask how my book is coming along.
Jeff will read a chapter and give me a detailed critique and suggestions for improvements. My son Joshua will stay out of my
way for hours because he knows I am working on the book. My
friends—Paula Bell, Emily Meyer, Roslyn Weinberger, Barry
Kohn, Barbara Masnick, Bill Taylor, Barbara Julius, Joyce
Lewis—and my parents, Charlotte and Sirol Katz, were consistently loving and supportive to me.

Several people, whose concern and involvement throughout
the writing of this book have sustained me, I truly thank and
acknowledge:

Alice Kohn, who in the process of being my mainstay,
discovered that she could co-parent within her marriage;

Jeff Galper, for his incisive comments, helpful criticisms,
general all around support, and for being the father of my
child;

Joshua Galper, a prince of a person, whose love lights up my
life;

Carolyn Kott Washburne, my dearest friend and colleague;

Carl Hirsch, who knew me when, and who has encouraged
and supported my work in untold ways;

Lawrence Teacher, whose vision made this book possible;
and

Peter John Dorman, a very special editor and friend.

Thank you.

Index

About the Author

Miriam Galper is the Executive Director of HELP, Inc., a drug and alcohol treatment center and mental health facility in Philadelphia. She holds a Master of Science in Social Work from Columbia University and is a member of the National Association of Social Workers and the Academy of Certified Social Workers. Ms. Galper was a staff person for four years at Women in Transition, also in Philadelphia, and was a member of the collective that wrote *Women in Transition*. She was also general editor of *For Better, For Worse*. Ms. Galper has appeared extensively on radio and television—including the nationally syndicated *Phil Donahue Show*—and gives workshops and lectures in the areas of custody, separation, and divorce. She has appeared as an expert witness in court custody cases, and has testified before state judiciary committees investigating joint custody.